# ScottForesman
# In Contact 1

**CHARLES RAHT**
Institute of North American Studies
Barcelona, Spain

**BARBARA R. DENMAN**
Prince George's County Adult Education Program
Prince George's County, Maryland

**N. ELIZABETH LAVIE**
The British Council

**SANDRA J. BRIGGS**
San Mateo Union High School District
San Mateo, California

## SERIES CONSULTANTS

**JAMES E. PURPURA**
Institute of North American Studies
Barcelona, Spain

**DIANE PINKLEY**
Institute of North American Studies
Badalona, Spain

 ScottForesman
*A Division of* HarperCollins*Publishers*

I would like to thank my family, friends and colleagues who have helped me to complete this book. Similarly, thanks are due to the editorial staff of Scott, Foresman and Company from whom I received considerable guidance throughout the project. Most of all, I want to thank Kevin Rimmington who gave me advice, support, and encouragement throughout this seemingly endless endeavor: ta, Kev.

Charles Raht

I would like to thank Mark, Charles, Alex, and Teddy for their help and support during this project. I would also like to thank the staff at Scott, Foresman and Company: Tim Collins for getting me into this, and Judy Mendel and Chris Williams for getting me through it.

Barbara R. Denman

## CONSULTING REVIEWERS

Anna Marie Amudi, *Dhahran Ahliyya Schools*
Dammam, Saudi Arabia

Augusto Baratau, *American Language School*
Guayaquil, Ecuador

Antonio Cervellino, *Chilean Ministry of Education*
Santiago, Chile

Manuel C. R. Dos Santos, *ELT Author/Consultant*
Curitiba, Brazil

Tracy Caldwell Gavilanes, *Pontificia Universidad Católica del Ecuador*
Quito, Ecuador

Barbara A. Encinas, *Mesa Community College*
Mesa, Arizona

Miriam García de Bermúdez, *Universidad de Costa Rica*
San Jose, Costa Rica

Stephen Gudgel, *Institute of North American Studies*
Barcelona, Spain

Mario Herrera Salazar, *Director, Language Center of the Normal Superior of Nuevo Leon*
Monterrey, Mexico

Carlos Alberto Hoffmann de Mendonça, *Colegio Pedro II*
Rio de Janeiro, Brazil

Titika Magaliou, *Athens College*
Athens, Greece

Juana I. Marín, *Catedratica, Escuela Oficial de Idiomas de Madrid*
Madrid, Spain

Ricardo F. Marzo, *Director, ELS-Peru*
Lima, Peru

Lourdes Montoro, M.A. (English Philology), *Escola Oficial d'Idiomes*
Barcelona, Spain

Diane E. Özbal, *Robert College*
Istanbul, Turkey

Jose Javier Preciado Ceseña, *Universidad Nacional Autonoma de Mexico, Centro Universitario Mexico*
Mexico City, Mexico

Issam Safady, *University of Jordan, English Department*
Amman, Jordan

Christine Zaher, M.A., M. Ed., *The American University in Cairo*
Cairo, Egypt

Abla Zuraykat, *Ahliyyah School for Girls*
Amman, Jordan

We wish to thank the following people for their assistance in preparing these materials.

Maria Frias, *Colegio/Instituto Bachillerato Ramiro de Maeztu*
Madrid, Spain

Ramon Palencia, *Instituto Bachillerato Maria Zambrano*
Madrid, Spain

Colegio Viaro
Barcelona, Spain

Bonnie Baker, John Hang, *Institute of North American Studies*
Barcelona, Spain

Illustration and photography credits will be found on page 108.

ISBN: 0-673-19524-4

# CONTENTS

## A. Greetings

**1.** Good morning, Lisa.

Good morning.

**3.** Hello, Mr. Lewis.

Good evening, Ms. Roberts.

**2.** Good afternoon, class.

Good afternoon, Mr. Lewis.

**4.** Hello, Jeff.

Hi, Lisa.

## B. *Things to Know*

1. a book
2. an eraser
3. paper
4. a pen
5. a pencil
6. chalk
7. a blackboard
8. a door
9. a window
10. a desk
11. a backpack
12. a briefcase
13. a bus
14. a car
15. a plane

A: What's this?
B: It's a book.

1.

2.

3.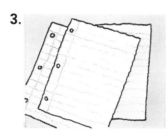

4.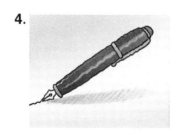

5.

6.

7.

8.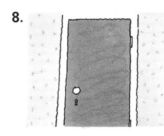

9.

10.

11.

12.

13.

14.

15.

## C. *The Alphabet*

A B C D E F G H I J K L M N O P Q R S T U V W X Y Z
a b c d e f g h i j k l m n o p q r s t u v w x y z

## D. *Things to Do*

**1.** Stand up.

**4.** Open your book.

**7.** Look at picture 1.

**2.** Sit down.

**5.** Close your book.

**8.** Listen.

**3.** Raise your hand.

**6.** Go to the door.

**9.** Repeat. Book.

## E. *Things to Say*

**1.**

**2.**

## WARM UP

### A. *What Does She Do?*

Look at number 1. What does she do?

She's a student.

### B. *What Does He Do?*

Look at number 8. What does he do?

He's a teacher.

### C. *What Do You Do?*

Very good! And what do you do?

I'm a student.

**EXERCISE 1:** *What Does She Do? What Does He Do?*

*Ask and answer the questions in A and B. Use these words.*

**1.** a student      **3.** a doctor      **5.** a nurse      **7.** a dentist      **9.** an actor

**2.** an actress      **4.** a secretary      **6.** a taxi driver      **8.** a teacher      **10.** a pilot

## D. *Where Are You From?*

 **EXERCISE 2:** *Where Are You From?*

*Ask and answer the questions in D.*

**1.** Ed Duran
San Antonio, Texas

**3.** Alida Alvarez
Cali, Colombia

**5.** Davut Basaran
Izmir, Turkey

**7.** Aldo Sanchez
Malaga, Spain

**2.** Marie Bonnard
Tours, France

**4.** Samira Arnout
Tanta, Egypt

**6.** Luis Alonso
Veracruz, Mexico

**8.** Diana Todd
Chicago, Illinois

## E. *Yes or No?*

**1.** MRS. SMITH: What's his name?
　　MR. SMITH: Luis Alonso.
　　MRS. SMITH: Is he from Chicago?
　　MR. SMITH: No, he's not.
　　　　　　　He's from Veracruz.

**2.** MRS. SMITH: What's her name?
　　MR. SMITH: Diana Todd.
　　MRS. SMITH: Is she a secretary?
　　MR. SMITH: Yes, she is.

**EXERCISE 3:**
*Tell About the People*

Ask and answer the questions in E.
Talk about the people in Exercise 2.
Talk about the students in your class.

**EXERCISE 4:** *Tell About Yourself*

**A.** *Fill in the form.*

My name is _____

I'm a/an _____

I'm from _____

**B.** *Introduce yourself to the class.*

## CONVERSATIONS

> Good afternoon, ladies and gentlemen, and welcome to the show. I'm Bill Wilson. Let's meet Player One. Player One, please stand up.

**A.**
BILL: What's your name, Player One?
CLARE: My name is Clare Taylor.
BILL: Nice to meet you, Clare.
CLARE: Nice to meet you, too, Bill.
BILL: Where are you from, Clare?
CLARE: I'm from Haywood, Wisconsin.
BILL: And what do you do in Haywood?
CLARE: I'm a bus driver.
BILL: Well, welcome to the show.
CLARE: Thanks.

**B.**
BILL: Are you ready for word one?
CLARE: Yes, I am.
BILL: Audience, are you ready?
AUDIENCE: Yes, we are!
BILL: OK. Word one is *window*.
Please spell *window*.
CLARE: W-I-N-D-O-W.
BILL: That's right! Very good!
Word two is *briefcase*. Please
spell *briefcase*.
CLARE: B-R-E-I-F-C-A-S-E.
BILL: Ohhhh. I'm sorry. That's wrong.
Audience, please spell *briefcase*.
AUDIENCE: B-R-I-E-F-C-A-S-E!
BILL: Very good, audience.
Clare, thanks for being on the show.
CLARE: Thank you, Bill.

# VOCABULARY

| Occupations | Expressions | | Where? | Pronouns |
|---|---|---|---|---|
| an actor | Nice to meet you. | a name | | I |
| an actress | What do you do? | a number | | you |
| a dentist | What does he/she do? | a question | from | she |
| a doctor | | a taxi | | he |
| a (bus) driver | | a word | and | it |
| a nurse | | | | we |
| a pilot | | no | answer | they |
| a secretary | | yes | ask | |
| a student | | | be: am/is/are | my |
| a teacher | | ready | introduce | your |
| | | right | spell | her |
| | | wrong | | his |

## EXERCISE 5: *Vocabulary Check*

*Ask and answer questions. Use **he** or **she**.*

A: What does she do?
B: She's an actress.

1.
4.
7.

2.
5.
8.

3.
6.
9.

# WORD FOR WORD

## Numbers

| 1 | 2 | 3 | 4 | 5 | 6 | 7 | 8 | 9 | 10 |
|---|---|---|---|---|---|---|---|---|---|
| one | two | three | four | five | six | seven | eight | nine | ten |

| 11 | 12 | 13 | 14 | 15 |
|---|---|---|---|---|
| eleven | twelve | thirteen | fourteen | fifteen |

**EXERCISE 6:** *What Are the Numbers?*

6    A: What's six and two?
+2   B: Six and two is eight.

**a.** 4    **b.** 7    **c.** 3    **d.** 9    **e.** 2    **f.** 6    **g.** 8    **h.** 10    **i.** 1
+8        +1        +12       +5        +11       +4        +7         +3          +9

 **GRAMMAR**

## A. *The Simple Present Tense: The Verb To Be*

**I am** from Mexico City.
**You are not** from Mexico City.
**He/She/It is** from New York.

**We are** from Monterrey.
**You are not** from Monterrey.
**They are** from Los Angeles.

note

| Contractions | | | | | | |
|---|---|---|---|---|---|---|
| I + am = I'm | we + are = we're |
| you + are = you're | you + are = you're |
| he + is = he's | they + are = they're |
| she + is = she's | |
| it + is = it's | |

## B. *The Simple Present Tense: Yes/No Questions with To Be*

Mr. Brown **is** a teacher.
**Is** he an actor?
Yes, he **is**./No, **he's not.**/No, he **isn't.**

The Perezes **are** from Madrid.
**Are** the Cortezes from Barcelona?
Yes, they **are**./No, **they're not.**/No, they **aren't.**

note

| Contractions | | |
|---|---|---|
| is + not = isn't |
| are + not = aren't |

ED:    Are you from France?
ALDO:  No, I'm not.
       I'm from Spain.
ED:    Are you a pilot?
ALDO:  Yes, I am.

DIANA:  Is Luis from Mexico?
DAVUT:  Yes, he is.
DIANA:  Is he an actor?
DAVUT:  No, he's not.
        He's a dentist.

MARIE:  Are Ed and Diana from
        the United States?
ALIDA:  Yes, they are.
MARIE:  Are they from Dallas?
ALIDA:  No, they're not.

**EXERCISE 7:** *Yes or No?*

*Are they from England or the United States? Ask and answer questions.*

A: Look at number 1. Is she from England?

B: No, she's not.

1. Meryl Streep    2. Elvis Presley    3. Princess Diana    4. Phil Collins    5. Madonna    6. Paul McCartney

**EXERCISE 8:** *Are You from Turkey?*

*Write the correct words on the lines.*

ED: **1.** _____ you from Turkey?

DAVUT: **2.** Yes, _____ .

LUIS: **3.** _____ Ed from Texas?

ALDO: **4.** Yes, _____ .

DIANA: **5.** _____ Alida from Bogota?

MARIE: **6.** No, _____ .        **7.** _____ from Cali.

SAMIRA: **8.** _____ Marie and Aldo from Canada?

ALIDA: **9.** No, _____ .        **10.** _____ from Europe.

## C. *The Simple Present Tense: Information Questions with To Be*

| | |
|---|---|
| **What is** your name?<br>My name **is** Clara.<br>**What is** his name?<br>His name **is** Ed. | **Where are** you from?<br>I **am** from New York.<br>**Where are** they from?<br>They **are** from Asia. |

| Contractions | | | | |
|---|---|---|---|---|
| What | + | is | = | What's |
| Where | + | is | = | Where's |

**EXERCISE 9:** *Getting Information*

A. *Read the answer. Write the question.*

ED: **1.** _____ ?
MARIE: Her name is Samira.

ED: **2.** _____ ?
MARIE: She's from Egypt.

ED: **3.** _____ ?
MARIE: His name is Aldo.

ED: **4.** _____ ?
MARIE: He's from Spain.

ED: **5.** _____ ?
MARIE: He's a pilot.

B. *Work with a partner. Ask and answer the questions about students in your class.*

**LISTENING**

*Prelistening*

Read the answers in Exercise 10. What is the question for each answer?

 **EXERCISE 10:** *What's the Answer?*

*Listen to the question. Circle the correct answer.*

**1.** Fine, thank you.    Good afternoon.
**2.** She's from Lima.    She's a doctor.
**3.** His name is Mario.    He's from California.

**4.** I'm a student.    I'm fine.
**5.** I'm a dentist.    I'm from Dublin.

 **PRONUNCIATION**

**EXERCISE 11:** *Yes/No Questions and Answers*

*Listen and repeat.*

**1.** Are you a teacher?
No, I'm a student.

**2.** Is she an actress?
No, she's not.
She's a nurse.

**3.** Is he a doctor?
Yes, he's a doctor.

**4.** Are you from Texas?
Yes, I am.
I'm from San Antonio.

**5.** Are they from Spain?
No, they're from France.

**EXERCISE 12:** *Question or Answer?*

*Listen to the sentence. Is it a question or an answer? Circle the correct word.*

**1.** question   answer
**2.** question   answer
**3.** question   answer

**4.** question   answer
**5.** question   answer
**6.** question   answer

**SPEAKING**

**A.** Circle the best answers.

**B.** Work with a partner. Read the conversation aloud.

**C.** Work with a partner. Ask the questions. Tell about yourselves.

**1.** Good morning.

Good morning.
Good evening.

**2.** How are you?

Nice to meet you.
I'm fine, thank you.

**3.** What's your name?

My name is Jim Hanson.
I'm from Illinois.

**4.** Where are you from?

I'm a pilot.
I'm from Chicago.

**5.** What do you do?

I'm sorry.
I'm a student.

**READING**

### Prereading

A pen pal writes letters to you, and you write letters to him or her. Are you a pen pal?

 **EXERCISE 13:**
*Understanding the Reading*

*Answer the questions.*

1. Where is Masao from?
2. What does Masao do?

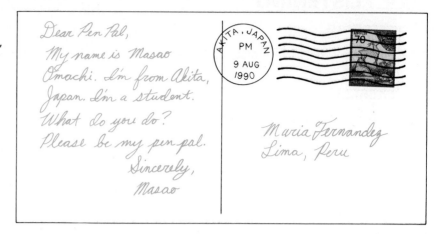

*Dear Pen Pal,*
*My name is Masao*
*Omachi. I'm from Akita,*
*Japan. I'm a student.*
*What do you do?*
*Please be my pen pal.*
*Sincerely,*
*Masao*

AKITA, JAPAN
PM
9 AUG
1990

*Maria Fernandez*
*Lima, Peru*

 **WRITING**

**A. Model.**
Finish the letter.
Use these words.

**Maria Fernandez**
**Lima, Peru**
**teacher**

Dear Masao,

My name is _____ . I'm a

_____ . I'm from _____ .

It's nice to be your pen pal.

Sincerely,

**B. Prewriting. Writing.** Write a letter to a pen pal about yourself. What do you want to say? Look at the model. Use another sheet of paper.

**C. Revising. Presenting.** Read your letter. Is everything correct? Make any corrections. Now write the final copy.

 **SPEAK OUT!**

### Game Shows
**A.** Work with a partner. You are Bill and Clare from page 7. Play "Spell It Right!" Take turns.

**B.** Work with another partner. Play "What's the Number?" Ask, "What is two and five?" Take turns.

---

# UNIT 2 Business or Vacation?

**WARM UP**

What do they do?
Where do they work?

**EXERCISE 1:** *What Do They Do? Where Do They Work?*

*Look at the pictures. Write the numbers.*

**a.** _____ They're doctors.
They work at a hospital.

**b.** _____ They're nurses.
They work at a hospital, too.

**c.** _____ They're musicians.
The boy plays the drums.
The girl plays the guitar.

**d.** _____ They're clerks.
They don't work in an office.
They work in a hotel.

**e.** _____ The man is an actor.
The woman is an actress.
They work in a theater.

**f.** _____ He's a teacher.
He doesn't work at a school.
He works in a theater, too.

**g.** _____ She's a pilot.
She works on a plane.

**h.** _____ They're secretaries.
They work in an office.

---

**UNIT 2  BUSINESS OR VACATION?**                                      13

# CONVERSATIONS

## A. At the airport in London

KENJI: Is this the flight to Chicago?
CLERK: Yes, it is. Do you have your ticket?
KENJI: Yes, I do. Here it is.
CLERK: Thank you. Is your name Kenji Miula?
KENJI: Well, my first name is Kenji, but my last name is Miura.
CLERK: Spell your last name, please.
KENJI: M-I-U-R-A.
CLERK: Thank you. Do you live in London?
KENJI: Yes, I do. I study English here.
CLERK: OK, Mr. Miura. Do you have a suitcase?
KENJI: Yes, I do. I have a guitar and a backpack, too. Here they are.
CLERK: Thank you. Have a nice flight.
KENJI: Thanks.

## B. On the plane

ATTENDANT: Ladies and gentlemen, may I have your forms, please?
KENJI: Excuse me. What does *occupation* mean?
ATTENDANT: What do you do, sir?
KENJI: I'm a student.
ATTENDANT: Then your occupation is "student."
KENJI: And what about *nationality?*
ATTENDANT: Where are you from?
KENJI: Japan.
ATTENDANT: Then write "Japanese."
KENJI: Thank you.
ATTENDANT: You're welcome.

## C. At the airport in Chicago

CLERK: Name, please?
KENJI: Kenji Miura. M-I-U-R-A.
CLERK: What's your occupation, Mr. Miura?
KENJI: I'm a student.
CLERK: Are you on business?
KENJI: No, I'm not. I'm on vacation.
CLERK: What's your address in Chicago?
KENJI: 15 School Street.
CLERK: Is that a hotel?
KENJI: No, it's not. My friend Dr. Yatabe lives there.
CLERK: Thank you, Mr. Miura. Welcome to Chicago. Have a nice vacation.
KENJI: Thanks.

 **EXERCISE 2:**
*Understanding*
*the Conversations*

*Fill in this form for Kenji.*

Name _____ _____
               FIRST                           LAST
Occupation _____
Nationality _____
Address in the US? _____ _____
                              STREET                    CITY
On business or vacation? _____

# VOCABULARY

**Places**
airport
city
hospital
hotel
office
school
street
theater

address
business
drum
form
guitar
piano
suitcase
ticket
vacation

**People**
boy
clerk
friend
girl
man
musician
woman

fill in/fills in
have/has
live/lives
mean/means
play/plays
speak/speaks
work/works

**Expressions**
Excuse me.
Have a nice (afternoon).
Here it is./Here they are.
May I have (your form)?
You're welcome.

first
last

at
in
on

too

note

The book is **in**
the desk.

The book is **on**
the desk.

The teacher is **at**
the blackboard.

**EXERCISE 3:** *Where Do They Work?*

*Write the correct word on the line.*

**1.** He's a _____ . He works on a plane.

**2.** She's a doctor. She works at a _____ .

**3.** He's a _____ . He works at a school.

**4.** They're actors. They work in a _____ .

**5.** He's a _____ . He works on a bus.

**6.** She's a secretary. She works in an _____ .

**7.** She's an _____ . She works in a theater.

**8.** She's a pilot. She works on a _____ .

**9.** They're _____ . They work in a hotel.

**10.** She's a nurse. She works at a _____ .

---

**EXERCISE 4: *Where Are They?***

Look at the picture. Write *in, on* or *at* on the line.

1. The boy is _____ the blackboard.

2. The books are _____ the desk.

3. The guitar is _____ the chair.

4. The paper is _____ the briefcase.

5. The boy is _____ his desk.

## WORD FOR WORD

### A. *Doers*

> A **musician** plays **music**.
> An English **student studies** English.
> A bus **driver drives** a bus.
> A French **speaker speaks** French.

**EXERCISE 5: *What Do They Do?***

1. What does a guitar player do?
2. What does an English teacher do?
3. What does a taxi driver do?
4. What does a music teacher do?
5. What does an office worker do?

### B. *Numbers*

| 16 | 17 | 18 | 19 | 20 |
|---|---|---|---|---|
| sixteen | seventeen | eighteen | nineteen | twenty |

## GRAMMAR

### A. *A/An*

| a teacher | an **a**ctress |
|---|---|
| a pilot | an **o**ffice |
| a doctor | an **e**raser |

**EXERCISE 6: *A or An?***

Say the word. Use *a* or *an*.

1. ticket    3. afternoon   5. evening   7. drum      9. answer
2. airport   4. friend      6. actor     8. vacation  10. picture

### B. *Singular and Plural Nouns*

a ticket

tickets

an actress

actresses

a secretary

secretaries

a taxi driver

taxi drivers

a man

men

a woman

women

**EXERCISE 7:** *Plural Nouns*

*Spell the plural forms of these nouns.*

| | | | | |
|---|---|---|---|---|
| **1.** clerk | **3.** address | **5.** nurse | **7.** piano player | **9.** city |
| **2.** man | **4.** bus driver | **6.** door | **8.** desk | **10.** woman |

## C. *The Simple Present Tense: Yes/No Questions and Answers*

I/You/We/They **work** in an office.
**Do** (you) **work** in a hotel?
Yes (I) **do.**/No, (I) **don't.**

**Does** he/she/it **play** the guitar?
Yes, (she) **does.**/No, (she) **doesn't.**

**EXERCISE 8:** *What Are the Right Verbs?*

*Circle the answers.*

1. With **I, you, we,** and **they,** use    do    does    don't    doesn't.

2. With **he, she,** and **it,** use    do    does    don't    doesn't.

**EXERCISE 9:** *Short Answers*

*Look at the picture.*
*Work with a partner.*
*Answer the questions.*

1. Does Kenji have his guitar?

2. Does he have his backpack?

3. Do the pilots have guitars?

4. Do the pilots have briefcases?

5. Does Kenji have a briefcase?

Do you have my backpack?

**EXERCISE 10:** *Questions*

A. *Read the questions in the form.*
   *Circle your answers.*

B. *Work with a partner. Ask the questions.*
   *Circle your partner's answers.*

| | | | | |
|---|---|---|---|---|
| Do you speak English? | yes | no | yes | no |
| Do you speak Greek? | yes | no | yes | no |
| Do you have a car? | yes | no | yes | no |
| Do you play the guitar? | yes | no | yes | no |
| Do you work in an office? | yes | no | yes | no |

## D. *The Simple Present Tense: Information Questions and Answers*

I/You/We/They **don't live** in Paris.
**Where do** (you) **live?**
(I) **live** in Tokyo.

He/She/It **doesn't live** in Chicago.
**Where does** (she) **live?**
(She) **lives** in Washington, DC.

I/You/We/They **don't have** a briefcase.
**What do** (you) **have?**
(I) **have** a backpack.

He/She/It **doesn't have** a piano.
**What does** (he) **have?**
(He) **has** a guitar.

EXERCISE 11: *What Are the Right Pronouns?*

Circle the correct answers.

Use **works, plays, spells** with    I    he    you    we    she    they    it

EXERCISE 12: *Making Introductions*

**A.** Write the correct form of the verb on the line.

**live        play        speak        work**

KENJI:    Hi, Junko. How are you?

JUNKO:    Fine, thanks. Kenji, this is my friend, Reiko. She's a musician. She
          **(1)** _____ at the theater. She **(2)** _____ the piano.

KENJI:    Nice to meet you, Reiko. I'm a musician, too. I **(3)** _____ the guitar.

REIKO:    Nice to meet you, too. Do you **(4)** _____ in Chicago?

KENJI:    No, I don't. I'm here on vacation. I **(5)** _____ in London. Oh. Here
          are my friends Hiroko and Anna. They **(6)** _____ in Chicago. Hiroko
          **(7)** _____ at a hospital. He's a doctor. Anna is a secretary. She
          **(8)** _____ at the hospital, too.

JUNKO:    Hello, Anna. Do you **(9)** _____ English?

ANNA:     Of course. I'm from New York. I don't **(10)** _____ Japanese!

**B.** Work with two other students. Introduce them to each other.

# LISTENING

*Prelistening*

Look at the pictures in Exercise 13. Name the places.

EXERCISE 13: *Where Do They Work?*

Listen to the sentences. Write the correct name on the line.

**Tom        Allen        Barbara        Maria        Ann        Mario**

1. _____Mario_____

2. _____

3. _____

4. _____

5. _____

6. _____

**PRONUNCIATION**

EXERCISE 14: *Listening to Plural Nouns*

*Plural nouns end in -s or -es.*
*Listen and repeat.*

| **1.** | | **2.** | | **3.** | |
|---|---|---|---|---|---|
| clerks | streets | forms | doors | actresses | offices |
| flights | desks | friends | pens | classes | nurses |

 **SPEAKING**

**A.** Draw a line from the question to the correct answer.

Is he from England?          He's from Australia.

Where is he from?          He has his backpack.

Does he have a suitcase?          No, he's not.

What does he have?          No, he doesn't.

Excuse me. Do you have a pen?          Here you are.

Do you have a pencil?          No, I don't have a pen. Sorry.

May I have one, please?          You're welcome.

Thanks.          Yes, I do. I have two.

**B.** Work with a partner. Read the conversations aloud.

**C.** Work with a partner. What does your partner have? (A pen? A pencil? An eraser? A backpack? A briefcase?) Tell the class.

 **READING**

*Prereading*

Look at Exercise 12. Where do Hiroshi and Anna live? What does Hiroshi do? What does Anna do?

### The Yatabes

Hiroshi and Anna Yatabe live in Chicago. Their address is 15 School Street. They live on the second floor.

Hiroshi is from Japan. He speaks English and Japanese. He works at Mercy Hospital. He's a doctor.

Anna works at Mercy Hospital, too, but she's not a doctor. She's a secretary. Her office is on the first floor. She fills in forms for the doctors and nurses. Anna is from New York. She speaks English. She understands some Japanese, but she doesn't speak it very well.

Hiroshi and Anna are musicians, too. Hiroshi plays the guitar, and Anna plays the piano. They play music or listen to music on the radio every night after work. They're tired, but they have a good time.

**second floor**

**first floor**

**radio**

---

**EXERCISE 15:**
*Understanding the Reading*

*Fill in this form for Hiroko.*

```
NAME _____ _____
            FIRST                      LAST

OCCUPATION _____

WORKS AT _____

NATIONALITY _____

SPEAKS _____

ADDRESS _____ _____
              STREET                  CITY
```

 **WRITING**

**A. Model.** Read this form. Write 5 sentences about Maria. (Look at the story about Hiroko and Anna.)

**B. Prewriting. Writing.** Look at the form. What's your name? What's your occupation? What's your address? What's your nationality? What languages do you speak? Write five sentences about yourself.

**C. Revising. Presenting.** Read your sentences. Is everything correct? Make the corrections. Write the final copy.

```
NAME _____ Maria _____   _____ Puzzo _____
            FIRST                   LAST

OCCUPATION _____ Teacher _____

WORKS AT _____ Del Mar High School _____

NATIONALITY _____ Venezuelan _____

SPEAKS _____ Spanish, Portuguese _____

ADDRESS __ 7 Hacienda Heights __  ____ Del Mar ____
              STREET                   CITY
```

**SPEAK OUT!**

**A. Introductions**
Work with a partner. Tell your partner about yourself. Give the information from the form in the Writing section. Tell the class about your partner.

**B. Survey**
Make an address book for your class. Ask the other students for their names, addresses, occupations, and nationalities. Check your information with a partner.

# UNIT 3 Family Trees

## WARM UP

### A. Family Tree

Mike is Janet's father.
Barbara is Janet's mother.
Cathy is Janet's sister.
Ken is Janet's brother.

Mike is Barbara's husband.
Barbara is Mike's wife.
Ken is Barbara and Mike's son.
Janet and Cathy are Barbara
    and Mike's daughters.

Rosa is Janet's grandmother.
John is Janet's grandfather.
Janet and Cathy are Carol and
    Charles's granddaughters.
Ken is Carol and Charles's
    grandson.

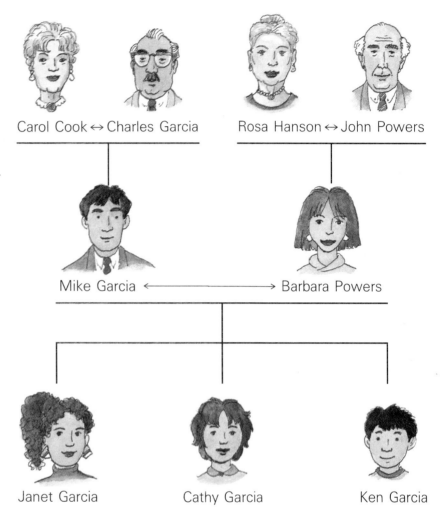

Carol Cook ↔ Charles Garcia          Rosa Hanson ↔ John Powers

Mike Garcia ⟵⟶ Barbara Powers

Janet Garcia          Cathy Garcia          Ken Garcia

 **EXERCISE 1:** *Tell About Yourself*

**A.** *Fill in the form.*

**B.** *Work with a partner. Ask and answer questions about your families.*

A: What's your mother's name?
B: My mother's name is Susan.
   What's your mother's name?
A: My mother's name is Laura.

1. My mother's name is _____

2. My father's name is _____

3. My grandmothers' names are _____

4. My grandfathers' names are _____

5. *(Check the true sentences. Write the numbers.)*

☐ I don't have a brother.          ☐ I don't have a sister.

☐ I have one brother.          ☐ I have one sister.

☐ I have _____ brothers.          ☐ I have _____ sisters.

## B. *What Can They Do?*

It can fly,
but it can't swim.
It can talk.

It can swim,
but it can't fly.
It can't talk.

They can swim and fly.
Can they walk?
Yes they can.

It can't swim or fly.
Can it walk?
No, it can't.

1. sing
2. drive a bus
3. read
4. dance
5. ride a bike
6. run
7. swim
8. write
9. type
10. walk

**2.**

**5.**

**8.**

**3.**

**6.**

**9.**

**1.**

**4.**

**7.**

**10.**

 **EXERCISE 2:** *Can You Sing?*

*Work with a partner. Ask and answer questions.*

A: Can you sing?
B: Yes, I can. Can you drive a bus?
A: No, I can't.

## CONVERSATIONS

leaves

stalk

RHUBARB

**A.** **TEACHER:** Class, this is Professor Darla Williams. Professor Williams goes to schools and talks about plants. This morning, Professor Williams's talk is about rhubarb.

**PROFESSOR:** Good morning, class. This is *Rheum rhabarbarum* or rhubarb. Rhubarb is a very interesting plant.

**KEN:** Excuse me, Professor. I can't spell *rhubarb*. Please write it on the blackboard.

**PROFESSOR:** Of course. It's R-H-U-B-A-R-B. Can you read it?

**KEN:** Yes, I can. Thank you.

Pie:

**B.** **PROFESSOR:** Listen, class. Rhubarb is poisonous.

**MARIA:** Excuse me, Professor. Rhubarb isn't poisonous. My grandmother makes rhubarb pies. We eat the pies, and we aren't dead!

**PROFESSOR:** So, rhubarb is poisonous, but your grandmother's pies aren't poisonous. I can explain. Does your grandmother cook the stalks or the leaves?

**MARIA:** She cooks the stalks.

**PROFESSOR:** That's very important. You can cook and eat rhubarb stalks, but you can't eat the leaves.

**MARIA:** That's very interesting. Thank you, Professor Williams.

### EXERCISE 3:
### *Understanding the Conversations*

*Answer the questions.*

1. What is the professor's name?
2. Can the professor spell *rhubarb*?
3. What does Maria's grandmother make?
4. Can you eat the leaves of rhubarb?
5. Is rhubarb interesting? Explain.

### EXERCISE 4: *True or False?*

*Read the sentence. Circle **T** for true (correct) or **F** for false (not correct). Explain.*

(T)  F   A bike can't fly.

1. T  F   Plants can read.
2. T  F   Rhubarb is a plant.
3. T  F   A pilot drives a bus.
4. T  F   My father's wife is my sister.
5. T  F   Five and six is eleven.

## VOCABULARY

| | | |
|---|---|---|
| bike | make | *Family* |
| pie | read | father |
| plant | ride | son |
| | run | sister |
| false | sing | husband |
| important | swim | grandfather |
| interesting | talk | grandson |
| true | type | mother |
| | walk | daughter |
| that | write | brother |
| | | wife/wives |
| cook | can/can't | grandmother |
| dance | | granddaughter |
| do | but | |
| drive | or | |
| eat | | |
| explain | about | |
| fly | | |

**WORD FOR WORD**

## A. *This/That*

A: What's this?
B: It's a pen.

A: What's that?
B: It's an eraser.

**EXERCISE 5:** *This/That*

*Ask and answer questions about the pictures.*

**1.**

**3.**

**5.**

**2.**

**4.**

**6.**

## B. *Talk and Speak*

Professor Williams **speaks** English.
She **talks** about plants.
This morning the professor's **talk** is about rhubarb.

## C. *Numbers*

| 21 | 32 | 43 | 54 | 65 |
|---|---|---|---|---|
| twenty-one | thirty-two | forty-three | fifty-four | sixty-five |
| 76 | 87 | 98 | 100 | 1,000 |
| seventy-six | eighty-seven | ninety-eight | one hundred | one thousand |

---

# G GRAMMAR

## A. *Can/Can't*

| |
|---|
| What **can** I/you/he/she/it/we/you/they **do?** <br> (They) **can swim.** <br> (He) **can't swim.** |
| **Can** (you) **swim?** <br> Yes, (I) **can.**/No, (I) **can't.** |

| |
|---|
| can + not = can't |

A: Can you ride that bike?
B: No, I can't.

A: Can I ride my bike here?
B: No, you can't. You can ride on Plant Street.

**EXERCISE 6:** *What Can You Do?*

*What can you do? Write an X on the line. Work with a partner. What can your partner do? Write an X on the line.*

**EXERCISE 7:** *Can or Can't?*

*Talk about your partner in Exercise 6. Make ten sentences.*

(Partner's Name) can swim.
(Partner's Name) can't type.

| | | I can | My partner can |
|---|---|---|---|
| **1.** | swim | _____ | _____ |
| **2.** | ride a bike | _____ | _____ |
| **3.** | fly a plane | _____ | _____ |
| **4.** | drive a car | _____ | _____ |
| **5.** | make a pie | _____ | _____ |
| **6.** | read Greek | _____ | _____ |
| **7.** | speak French | _____ | _____ |
| **8.** | type | _____ | _____ |
| **9.** | play the guitar | _____ | _____ |
| **10.** | dance | _____ | _____ |

## B. *And, But, Or*

| | | |
|---|---|---|
| **AND** | I can swim. <br> I can drive, too. <br> I can swim **and** drive. | Tom can speak English. <br> Laura can speak English, too. <br> Tom **and** Laura can speak English. |
| **BUT** | I can sing. <br> I can't dance. <br> I can sing, **but** I can't dance. | Tom can't cook. <br> Laura can cook. <br> Tom can't cook, **but** Laura can. |
| **OR** | I can't type. <br> I can't ride a bike. <br> I can't type **or** ride a bike. | Laura can't play the drums. <br> Laura can't play the guitar. <br> Laura can't play the drums **or** the guitar. |

**EXERCISE 8:** *And, But, Or*

*Talk about you and your partner in Exercise 6. Can you make five sentences? Use **and, but, or**.*

## C. *Possessive Nouns*

> David has a briefcase.
> Here is **David's** briefcase.
>
> I have two brothers.
> My **brothers'** names are Tom and Joe.
>
> Carl and Alison have a car.
> This is **Carl and Alison's** car.

| | |
|---|---|
| actress's | actresses' |
| secretary's | secretaries' |
| woman's | women's |
| man's | men's |

**EXERCISE 9:** *Brother's or Brothers'?*

*Spell the possessive form of these nouns.*

brother = brother's     B-R-O-T-H-E-R-apostrophe-S
brothers = brothers'     B-R-O-T-H-E-R-S-apostrophe

**1.** sister   **3.** cities   **5.** wife   **7.** nurse
**2.** sisters   **4.** city   **6.** wives   **8.** nurses

**EXERCISE 10:** *Charles's Family Tree*

*Fill in the names on the family tree.*

**1.** Melanie is Charles's mother.
**2.** Paul is Melanie's husband.
**3.** John is Paul's father.
**4.** Marian is John's wife.
**5.** Melanie is Linda's daughter.
**6.** Michael and John are Charles's grandfathers.
**7.** Tracy is Charles's sister.
**8.** Tracy's brothers' names are Charles and David.

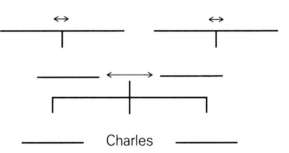

 **LISTENING**

### *Prelistening*

Look at the pictures. What can you do? What can't you do?

**EXERCISE 11:** *Can He Run?*

*Listen to each sentence. Circle **T** for true or **F** for false in each picture. Correct the false statements.*

**1. a.** T  F          **2. a.** T  F          **3. a.** T  F          **4. a.** T  F

**b.** T  F          **b.** T  F          **b.** T  F          **b.** T  F

**PRONUNCIATION**

**EXERCISE 12:** *Possessive Nouns*

*Possessive nouns sound like plural nouns.
Listen and repeat.*

| /s/ | /z/ | /əz/ |
|---|---|---|
| attendant's | mother's | actress's |
| clerk's | secretary's | class's |
| wife's | girl's | Charles's |

**EXERCISE 13:** *What's the Word?*

*Listen. Circle the correct word.*

**1.** actor    actor's    **5.** woman    woman's
**2.** brother   brother's  **6.** nurse    nurse's
**3.** dentist   dentist's  **7.** pilot    pilot's
**4.** friend    friend's   **8.** sister   sister's

 **SPEAKING**

**A.** Make conversations. Number the sentences in the correct order.

**1.** ____ Yes, I do. I have two brothers.
____ They're students.
____ What are your brothers' names?
____ What do they do?
____ Mark, do you have a brother?
____ Raymond and Nicholas.

**2.** ____ Her name is Julie.
____ No, she can't play the piano, but she can play the guitar.
____ Helen, do you have a sister?
____ Can she play the piano?
____ Yes, I do.
____ What's your sister's name?

**B.** Work with a partner. Read the conversations aloud.

**C.** Work with a partner. Does your partner have a brother or sister?
What is the brother's or sister's name? What can he or she do?

 **READING**

*Prereading*

Look at the pictures. Do you eat potatoes, tomatoes, or tobacco? What family is the reading about?

### A Plant Family

Do you eat tomatoes and potatoes? Tomato and potato plants are in the nightshade family. *Atropa belladonna* or deadly nightshade is in that family. Deadly nightshade is very poisonous. You can die if you eat a deadly nightshade plant.

Tomato and potato plants are poisonous, too. You can eat potatoes and tomatoes, but you can't eat the leaves of these plants.

Tobacco is in the nightshade family, too. Tobacco leaves have nicotine in them. Nicotine is very poisonous. You can eat tobacco leaves if you cook them. You can smoke tobacco leaves, too, but doctors say, "Tobacco is poisonous. Don't smoke!"

**potato:**

**tomato:**

**die:** not live

**tobacco leaves:**

**Don't smoke:**

---

**EXERCISE 14:** *Understanding the Reading*

*Read the sentence. Circle **T** for true and **F** for false. Explain.*

**1.** T F Tomatoes, potatoes, and tobacco are in one family.
**2.** T F You can eat the leaves of the tomato plant.
**3.** T F You can't eat the leaves of the potato plant.
**4.** T F Tobacco leaves are poisonous.
**5.** T F Nicotine is in tomato leaves.

## WRITING

**A. Model.** Read this paragraph about Mouneer and his family.

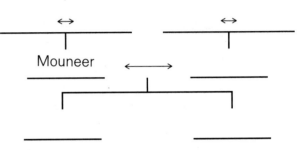

My name is Mouneer. I live in Cairo, Egypt. I'm a dentist. My wife's name is Mona. We have a son and a daughter. My daughter's name is Mouneera. My son's name is Sami. My father and mother live in Alexandria, Egypt. My father's name is Rauf. My mother's name is Fatima. Mona's mother and father live in Alexandria, too. Her mother's name is Aziza. Her father's name is Hassan.

**B.** Fill in Mouneer's family tree.

**C. Prewriting. Writing.** Look at Mouneer's family tree. Think about your family. Make a family tree for your family. Write a paragraph about your family.

**D. Rewriting. Presenting.** Read your paragraph. Is everything correct? Make the corrections. Write the final copy.

## SPEAK OUT!

**A. Interview**
Work with a partner. Make your partner's family tree.

**B. Survey**
What can the students in your class do? Write names after the words.

swim _____

ride a bike _____

type _____

drive a car _____

play the guitar _____

## WARM UP

What are they wearing? What color is it?

### EXERCISE 1: *What Are They Wearing?*

*Write the number of the correct picture next to the sentence.*

__1__ She's wearing a sweater.

_____ He's wearing a jacket.

_____ She's wearing a dress.

_____ He's wearing socks and shoes.

_____ He's wearing a T-shirt.

_____ She's wearing a skirt.

_____ He's wearing jeans.

_____ She's wearing a shirt.

### EXERCISE 2: *What Color Is It?*

*Match the clothes with the colors. Write the correct number.*

_____ It's green.

_____ It's red.

_____ They're blue.

_____ They're brown.

_____ It's yellow.

__1__ It's pink.

_____ It's white.

_____ It's purple.

### EXERCISE 3: *What Color?*

*Work with a partner. Ask and answer questions about the pictures.*

A: What's she wearing?
B: She's wearing a sweater.
A: What color is the sweater?
B: It's pink.

## CONVERSATIONS

**A.** **MRS. MILLER:** Excuse me. I want a shirt for my son. Do you have any boy's shirts on sale?

**SALESPERSON:** Yes, we do. These shirts are on sale. What color do you want?

**MRS. MILLER:** Blue. My son likes blue.

**SALESPERSON:** How about this shirt? Do you like it?

**MRS. MILLER:** Well, *I* like it, but it has short sleeves. My son likes long sleeves.

**SALESPERSON:** Here's one with long sleeves.

**MRS. MILLER:** This one's nice, but it's small. Do you have a large one?

**SALESPERSON:** Yes, we do.

**MRS. MILLER:** Good!

**B.** **MRS. MILLER:** Thank you. Now, can I buy shoes here, too?

**SALESPERSON:** I'm sorry. Style City doesn't have any shoes.

**MRS. MILLER:** Where can I buy some nice shoes?

**SALESPERSON:** Sal's is a good shoe store. It's across from Style City.

**MRS. MILLER:** I want a plant for my daughter, too. Is there a plant store in the mall?

**SALESPERSON:** Yes, there is. It's next to Style City.

**MRS. MILLER:** Is there a bookstore in the mall, too?

**SALESPERSON:** Yes, of course. There's a bookstore across from the plant store.

**MRS. MILLER:** And is there a music store?

**SALESPERSON:** Yes, it's between the shoe store and the bookstore.

**MRS. MILLER:** Thank you very much. I like this mall! Bye.

**EXERCISE 4:** *Understanding the Conversations*

*Answer the questions.*

**1.** What does Mrs. Miller want?
**2.** Does she want a small shirt for her son?
**3.** Does her son like long sleeves?
**4.** Where can she buy shoes?
**5.** Where is the bookstore in the mall?

## EXERCISE 5: *Treetown Mall*

*This is Treetown Mall.*
*Write the correct names on the stores.*

**WELCOME TO TREETOWN MALL!**

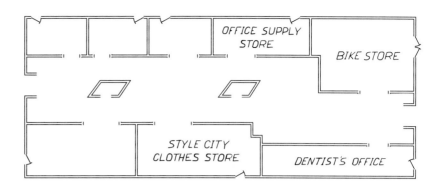

OFFICE SUPPLY STORE

BIKE STORE

STYLE CITY CLOTHES STORE

DENTIST'S OFFICE

## EXERCISE 6: *What Color is the Flag?*

*Work with a partner. Ask and answer about the flags.*

**Mexico**

A: What color is Mexico's flag?
B: It's green, white, and red.

**1.** Argentina

**4.** Spain

**2.** Egypt

**5.** Costa Rica

**3.** Japan

**6.** Venezuela

## WORD FOR WORD

### A. *Where Can You Buy It?*

You can buy shoes in **shoe stores**.
You can buy T-shirts in **T-shirt stores**.
You buy music, guitars, and pianos in **music stores**.

## EXERCISE 7: *Where Can You Shop For It?*

*Answer the questions.*

**1.** Where can you shop for plants?
**2.** Where can you shop for books?
**3.** Where can you shop for bikes?

# VOCABULARY

| | |
|---|---|
| large | **Colors** |
| long | black |
| short | blue |
| small | brown |
| | green |
| day | orange |
| mall | pink |
| salesperson | purple |
| sleeve | red |
| store | white |
| week | yellow |
| | |
| across from | **Clothes** |
| between | dress |
| for | jacket |
| next to | jeans |
| with | pants |
| without | shirt |
| | shoe |
| buy | skirt |
| come | sock |
| design | sweater |
| like | T-shirt |
| shop | |
| want | there |
| wear | these/those |
| | any/some |

*Expressions*
on sale
How about (this shirt)?
What's (she) wearing?
(She's) wearing (a coat).
What are (they) wearing?
(They're) wearing (jeans).

## B. *These/Those*

These books are blue. **Those** books are brown.

 **EXERCISE 8:** *These/Those*

*Ask and answer questions about the picture.*

A: What color are these cars?
B: These cars are red.
A: How about those cars? What color are they?
B: Those cars are green.

## C. *Days of the Week*

| Sunday | Monday | Tuesday | Wednesday | Thursday | Friday | Saturday |
|--------|--------|---------|-----------|----------|--------|----------|
| don't work | work at hotel | English class | work at hotel | English class | go to theater | don't work |

A: Do you work at the hotel?
B: Yes, I do.
A: What days do you work?
B: I work **on** Monday and Wednesday.
A: Do you work **on** Saturday?
B: No, I don't. I don't work **on** Saturday or Sunday.

 **GRAMMAR**

### A. *Adjectives*

| a | **blue** | shirt |
|------|-------------|--------|
| the | **interesting** | book |
| this | **wrong** | answer |

| the | **black** | shoes |
|-------|-------------|---------|
| these | **important** | classes |
| those | **green** | plants |

 **EXERCISE 9:** *Scrambled Sentences*

*Make sentences out of these words. Write them on a sheet of paper.*

**1.** jacket want I that blue
**2.** interesting have an you family
**3.** drives car Rodolfo a blue
**4.** city this good has schools
**5.** clothes Lori purple those likes

### B. *Any/Some*

Does the store have **any** blue shirts?
  Yes, it does. It has **some** blue shirts.
Does the store have **any** purple shirts?
  No, it doesn't. It **doesn't** have **any** purple shirts.

👤 **EXERCISE 10:** *Any or Some?*

*Circle the correct word.*

**1.** In **yes/no** questions, use          **any**     **some**

**2.** In sentences with **not**, use         **any**     **some**

**3.** In sentences without **not**, use     **any**     **some**

📖 **EXERCISE 11:** *What's on Sale?*

*Work with a partner. Ask and answer questions about the stores in Treetown Mall.*

A: Does the shoe store have any nurses' shoes on sale?
B: Yes, it does. It has some nurses' shoes on sale on Monday.
A: Great! I like sales!

B: Does the bike store have any French bikes on sale?
A: No, it doesn't have any French bikes, but it has some Italian bikes on sale.

**1.** clothes store/dresses
**2.** shoe store/running shoes
**3.** music store/guitars
**4.** bookstore/vacation books
**5.** plant store/tomato plants
**6.** bike store/Japanese bikes

**COME AND SHOP AT TREETOWN MALL!**

*Sal's Shoe Store*
Nurses' Shoes
on Sale MONDAY

**Brown's Bike Store**
**Italian Bikes on Sale SUNDAY**

*lack's ookstore*
Vacation Books on Sale FRIDAY

*reen Thumb Plant Store*
Tomato Plants ON SALE TUESDAY

*Good Music*
Spanish Guitars
on Sale THURSDAY

Shirts on Sale SATURDAY
*Style City Clothes*

## C. *There Is/There Are*

**There is** a shoe store in the mall.
**Is there** a clothes store in the mall?
Yes, **there is.**/No, **there's not.**/No, **there isn't.**

**There are** some doctor's offices in the mall.
**Are there** any theaters in the mall?
Yes, **there are.**/No, **there aren't.**

---

**UNIT 4   AT THE MALL**                                     **33**

EXERCISE 12: *Northland Mall*

*Work with a partner. Talk about Northland Mall.*

A: Excuse me. Is there a shoe store in Northland Mall?
B: Yes, there is. There's one between the bookstore and the T-shirt store.
A: Thanks.
B: You're welcome.

B: Excuse me. Is there a bike store in this mall?
A: No, there isn't.
B: Thank you.

| | |
|---|---|
| 1. shoe store | 7. clothes store |
| 2. bike store | 8. plant store |
| 3. theater | 9. bookstore |
| 4. T-shirt store | 10. doctor's office |
| 5. dentist's office | 11. school supply store |
| 6. office supply store | 12. music store |

| NORTHLAND MALL DIRECTORY |
|---|
| A   Tim's Bookstore |
| B   Maple's Shoe Store |
| C   Fred's T-Shirt Store |
| D   Green's School Supply Store |
| E   City Theater |
| F   Dentist's Office |
| G   White's Shoes |
| H   Northland Music |
| I    Northland Clothes Store |

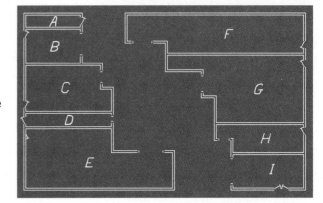

 **LISTENING**

**Prelistening**

Do you like designer clothes? What clothes designers do you know about?

 EXERCISE 13: *The Clothes Designer*

*Listen to the radio interview with a clothes designer. Circle the correct answers.*

| 1. What is the designer's name? | Nick | Phil | | | |
|---|---|---|---|---|---|
| 2. What colors does he like? | orange | yellow | black | red | white |
| 3. What clothes doesn't he design? | pants | shirts | sweaters | | |
| 4. Where is he from? | New York | Paris | Tokyo | | |
| 5. Where does he work? | New York | Paris | Tokyo | | |

 **PRONUNCIATION**

EXERCISE 14: *Short /š/*

*Listen and repeat.*

| | | | |
|---|---|---|---|
| **sh**e | **sh**irt | **sh**op | vaca**ti**on |
| **sh**oe | **sh**ort | musi**ci**an | |

EXERCISE 15: *Just for Fun*

*Listen to the sentence. Then say it.*

1. Teachers don't like short T-shirts.
2. She sells seashells by the seashore.

## SPEAKING

**A.** Read the chart. Write words on the lines under **hospitals.** What do you like? Write an **X.**

**B.** Work with a partner. What does your partner like? Write an **X.** Tell the class about you and your partner.

| Do you like . . . ? | I like . . . | My partner likes . . . . |
|---|---|---|
| purple clothes | | |
| malls | | |
| T-shirts | | |
| short skirts | | |
| school | | |
| hospitals | | |
| _____ | | |
| _____ | | |

## READING

*Prereading*

Look at the picture. What is the reading about? What is interesting about the picture?

## THINGS TO DO IN CANADA

THE MALL in West Edmonton, Alberta

Are you going on vacation in Canada? Come to the West Edmonton Mall. This indoor mall is very, very large. If you don't want to walk, you can go from store to store in a golf cart or a rickshaw.

You can shop in 828 stores. You can go to T-shirt stores, music stores, and souvenir stores. You can even buy a car!

Are you tired? Do you want to sit down and eat? There are 110 restaurants, from French to Chinese! (If you eat too much, there are 16 doctors to look at you!) Or you can go to the Fantasyland Hotel. It has 120 rooms.

Do you want to have some fun? There are waterslides and a roller coaster.

**Come to the West Edmonton Mall
with Your Family and Friends!**

**golf cart:**

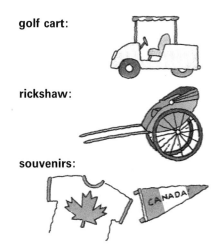

**rickshaw:**

**souvenirs:**

**restaurant:** You eat here.

**water slide:**

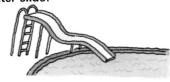

**roller coaster:**

**EXERCISE 16:** *Understanding the Reading*

*Answer the questions.*

**1.** Where is the mall?
**2.** Is the mall large or small?
**3.** Are there any music stores in the mall?

**4.** Where can you eat in the mall?
**5.** Where can you have some fun?

 **WRITING**

**A. Prewriting. Writing.** Work with a partner. You and your partner work for a new mall. What do you want in your mall? First, write ten ideas. What ideas do you and your partner like? Choose five. Write five sentences about your mall.

**B. Revising. Presenting.** Read the sentences. Are they correct? Make any corrections. Write the final copy.

**SPEAK OUT!**

**A. Find the Differences**
Work with a partner. Look at the two pictures. Find eight differences.

**B. You're the Designers**

**1.** Work with a partner. Design a street for shopping in your city. What stores do you want? Where are your stores? Write names on your stores.

**2.** Now work with another pair of partners. Look at your designs. Find five differences.

# UNIT 5 Let's Eat!

**WARM UP**

Are you hungry? Are you thirsty?

OUR HOT DOGS AND HAMBURGERS ARE GREAT!

THIRSTY? HAVE A SOFT DRINK

TEA

COFFEE

MILK

SUGAR

CAKES

PIES

BREAD

LETTUCE

TOMATOES

CHEESE

ONIONS

PIZZAS

MAKE YOUR SALAD HERE!

**EXERCISE 1:** *What Do You Want?*

*Look at the picture. What do you want to eat and drink?*

| I want<br>I'd like | a salad<br>a hamburger<br>a hot dog<br>a piece of cake<br>a piece of pizza | some tomatoes<br>some onions<br>some cheese<br>some lettuce | some coffee<br>some sugar<br>some milk |
|---|---|---|---|
| I don't want | a soft drink<br>a piece of pie | any onions<br>any tomatoes | any bread<br>any tea |

## CONVERSATIONS

**A. MARIO:** What do you want to do today?

**TONY:** Let's go to the mall. I need to buy a new shirt.

**MARIO:** OK. That's a good idea . . . Oh, no! I can't go today! Today is my sister's birthday. She's twenty-one years old.

**TONY:** So what's the problem?

**MARIO:** My sister wants a cake for her birthday. Let's make one.

**TONY:** What! Can you make a cake?

**MARIO:** Sure. My sister likes chocolate cake, so I make one every year. She says they're great.

**TONY:** Well, OK. What do we need? Do you have the ingredients ready?

**MARIO:** Yes, I do. We need some flour, some chocolate, and some sugar. I have them right here. I have butter, milk, and eggs, too.

**TONY:** Great! Let's make a cake!

**B. MARIO:** Happy birthday, Ellen. Do you like your cake?

**ELLEN:** It's great, Mario. Thanks!

**MARIO:** You're welcome, Ellen. But there's one problem.

**ELLEN:** What's that?

**MARIO:** Well, every year I make a cake, and every year you eat all of it. I'd like some, too!

**ELLEN:** I'm sorry. You can have a piece. Here's one.

**EXERCISE 2:** *Understanding the Conversations*

*Answer the questions.*

1. What does Tony need to buy at the mall?
2. What does Mario's sister like on her birthday?
3. What is Mario's sister's name?
4. What's Mario's problem?

**INGREDIENTS**

flour:

eggs:

butter:

EXERCISE 3: *I'm Hungry!*

*Work with a partner. Look at the pictures. Tell your partner what you want.*

A: What do you want?
B: I'm hungry. I'd like a cheese sandwich with tomatoes, please.

**1.**    **3.**    **5.**

**2.**    **4.**

# WORD FOR WORD

## A. *Months*

JANUARY FEBRUARY MARCH APRIL MAY JUNE JULY AUGUST SEPTEMBER OCTOBER NOVEMBER DECEMBER

## B. *How Old Are You?*

| How old **are you?** |
| **I'm** sixteen years old. |

| How old **are they?** |
| **They're** twenty years old. |

| How old **is he?** |
| **He's** fifteen years old. |

 EXERCISE 4: *How Old Are You?*

*How old are you? How old are your classmates? When are their birthdays? Make a graph.*

A: How old are you?
B: I'm sixteen years old.
A: When is your birthday?
B: It's in March.

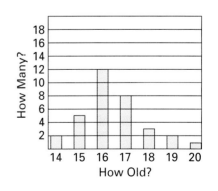

**GRAMMAR**

## A. *Count and Non-Count Nouns*

| Count | | Non-Count | |
|---|---|---|---|
| **a** hamburger | **some/any** hamburgers | milk | **some/any** milk |
| **an** egg | **some/any** eggs | coffee | **some/any** coffee |
| **a** piece of cake | **some/any** pieces of cake | lettuce | **some/any** lettuce |

A: Do you want **a** hot dog?
B: No, I don't want **a** hot dog.
 I want **a** hamburger with cheese.

A: Do you have **any** sandwiches?
B: No, I don't have **any** sandwiches,
 but I have **some** pizzas with onions.

A: Do you need **any** sugar?
B: No, I don't need **any** sugar, but
 I need **some** milk.

 note

A: I like **hamburgers** with cheese. Do you
 like **hamburgers?**
B: No, I don't. I don't like **hamburgers,** and
 I don't like cheese.

B: Do you want **a** hamburger?
A: Yes, I'd like **one,** please.
B: I have some onions. Do you want **some**
 on your hamburger?
A: No, thanks. I don't want **any.**

EXERCISE 5: *What Can I Get for You?*

**A.** *Write **a, an, some, any** or **X** (for no word) on the line.*

WAITER: What can I get for you?

TONY: I'm hungry! I want **(1)** _____ salad and **(2)** _____
 small pizza with **(3)** _____ onions.

MARIO: Can I have **(4)** _____ hamburger with **(5)** _____
 cheese, please? I'd like **(6)** _____ lettuce on it but
 I don't want **(7)** _____ tomatoes. I don't like
 **(8)** _____ tomatoes.

WAITER: Do you want coffee?

TONY: Yes, I'd like **(9)** _____ coffee, please.

WAITER: Do you want milk with that?

TONY: No, thanks. But I'd like **(10)** _____ sugar.

MARIO: I don't want **(11)** _____ coffee, thanks. I'd like
 **(12)** _____ tea with **(13)** _____ milk and **(14)** _____
 piece of chocolate cake.

**B.** *Work with a partner. You are a waiter and a customer.
What do you want to eat?*

## B. *Possessive Adjectives*

> **I** have **my** food.
> **You** have **your** food.
> **He** has **his** food.
> **She** has **her** food.
> **It** has **its** food.
> **We** have **our** food.
> **They** have **their** food.

 **note**

> Look at the adjectives with plural nouns.
>
> I have **my** idea.
> I have **my** ideas.
>
> They have **their** idea.
> They have **their** ideas.

📖 **EXERCISE 6:** *What's the Possessive Adjective?*

*Write the correct possessive adjective.*

I'm 17 years old. It's **(1)** _____ birthday. This is my brother. **(2)** _____ birthday is in June. That's my sister. **(3)** _____ birthday is in October.

ANN: Are you a taxi driver? Where's **(4)** _____ taxi?

TOM: Next to the bus. It's the one with **(5)** _____ door open.

ANN: We need a ride to the theater. We have **(6)** _____ guitars. Our friends need a ride, too. They have **(7)** _____ drums.

## C. *Infinitives with Like, Want, I'd like, and Need*

> I **like to eat** hamburgers.
> **What does** he like **to eat?**
> He **likes to eat** hot dogs.

> **What do** the women **want to drink?**
> **Do** they **want to drink** coffee?
> Yes, they **do.**/No, they **don't.**

> **I'd like to make** a cake.
> He **needs to buy** some eggs.

 **EXERCISE 7:** *Like or Don't Like?*

*What do you like to do? Write three things on a sheet of paper. What don't you like to do? Write three things. Find someone who likes and doesn't like to do the same things.*

A: Do you like to swim?
B: Yes, I do. Do you like to make cakes?
A: No, I don't.
B: What do you like to make?
A: I like to make pizzas.

---

## D. Let's

> Let's **eat.**
> **go** to the theater.
> **listen** to some music.

 **EXERCISE 8:** *What Do You Want to Make?*

**A.** *Work with a partner. You want to make some food. What do you want to make?*

A: Let's make some hamburgers.
B: No, thanks. I don't like hamburgers. Let's make a pizza.
A: OK. What do you like on your pizza?
B: I like cheese, tomatoes, and onions.
A: Great!

**B.** *Tell the class what you and your partner want to make.*

 **LISTENING**

### Prelistening

You work at a pizza restaurant. Look at the pictures. Describe the food. (Are the pizzas large or small? What's on them? What's in the salads?)

 **EXERCISE 9:**
*Pizza Connection*

*Ed is at work. He works at Pizza Connection. Look at the pictures and listen to the telephone conversations. Write the number of the conversation in the box in the correct picture.*

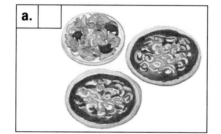

a.

c.

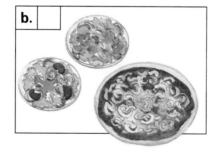

b.

 **PRONUNCIATION**

**EXERCISE 10:** *Hand or And?*

*Listen and repeat.*

**1.** hand   and     **4.** his   is
**2.** he     e       **5.** hi    I
**3.** how    ow      **6.** ham   am

**EXERCISE 11:** *Is There an /h/?*

*Listen. Circle the word you hear.*

**1.** his    is      **4.** hi    I
**2.** how    ow      **5.** ham   am
**3.** hand   and     **6.** he    e

# SPEAKING

**A.** *Read the chart. Write your own ideas for 9 and 10.*

**B.** *Find someone who . . .*

| 1. | doesn't drink tea. |
|---|---|
| 2. | likes to drink milk. |
| 3. | has some chocolate every day. |
| 4. | has a salad every evening. |
| 5. | likes chocolate cake. |
| 6. | likes to eat eggs in the morning. |
| 7. | doesn't like tomatoes. |
| 8. | needs to drink coffee in the morning. |
| 9. | |
| 10. | |

# READING

## *Prereading*

Look at the pictures. Look at the title of the reading. Where is the reading from? What is it about?

★ ★ ★ CHICAGO STAR ★ ★ ★

### CHICAGO'S GREAT FOOD FESTIVAL

Every year the city of Chicago has an outdoor food festival. Its name is Taste of Chicago. For eight days, you can't drive a car on Columbus Drive or Congress Drive, but you can walk, eat, and listen to music on those streets. The festival is open in the morning, afternoon, and evening. About 375,000 people go there every day.

At the festival, there is food from about eighty Chicago restaurants. You can eat quesadillas in a Mexican restaurant. Then you can have tempura in a Japanese restaurant. There is American food—hamburgers, hot dogs, and fried chicken—too.

What do people eat? Here are some interesting numbers from this year's festival: 55,000 hot dogs, 460,000 slices of pizza, 50,000 slices of cake, 102,000 egg rolls, and 27,000 kilos of French fries.

quesadillas:

tempura: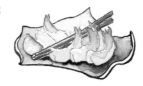

chicken:

egg roll:

French fries:

**EXERCISE 12:** *Scanning for Information*

*Scan the Reading. Look for a number or for a word with a capital letter. Answer the questions.*

**1.** Where is the food festival?
**2.** What can you eat at a Mexican restaurant?
**3.** What American food do they have at the festival?
**4.** Is there Japanese food at the festival?
**5.** What do 375,000 people do every day of the festival?

# WRITING

**Revising. Presenting.** This is an article for the *Chicago Star* about Taste of Chicago. You work at the *Chicago Star*. Look at the Reading on page 43 and this map to check the information. There are seven mistakes. Rewrite the article correctly.

You can eat some interesting food at Taste of Chicago. This year's festival has about eighty restaurants.

You can buy cheesecake at Harold's Chicken. Harold's Chicken is across from Guey Lon. There are hamburgers and tempura at Guey Lon. Salvador's Mexican Restaurant has very good quesadillas. It is between Barney's Market Club and Harold's Chicken. Little Quiapo is across from The Doggery. The Doggery has great egg rolls. Do you want a Greek salad? Go to It's Greek To Me. It's next to Little Quiapo and The Doggery.

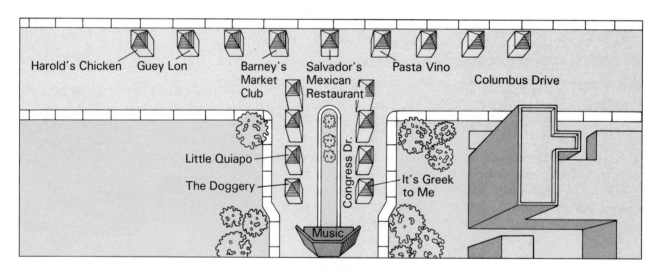

# SPEAK OUT!

**A. Food from Your Country**
Work in a small group. You are in an international food festival. You can make three things. What food from your country do you want to have? Tell the class.

**B. Food Festival**
Work in a small group. Organize a food festival. What food do you want at your food festival? What are the names of the restaurants? Draw a map. Report to the class.

## WARM UP

What are they doing? What are they wearing?

### EXERCISE 1: *What Are They Doing?*

A. *Look at the picture. Write the correct letter on the line.*

___A___ woman/getting a magazine

_____ **1.** reporter/following a man
_____ **2.** taxi driver/stopping behind the motorcycles
_____ **3.** girl/standing in front of the bookstore
_____ **4.** person/reading a newspaper
_____ **5.** boy and girl/waiting for the bus
_____ **6.** men/getting off their motorcycles
_____ **7.** spies/taking pictures

B. *Work with a partner. Ask and answer questions about the people.*

A: What is person A doing?
B: She's buying a magazine.

## CONVERSATIONS

Mr. Hanson is a reporter for *Today's Spy* magazine, and Mrs. Hanson writes spy stories. They aren't working today, but they're thinking about spies.

**A. MR. HANSON:** What are you doing, honey?

**MRS. HANSON:** I'm waiting for the mail carrier. What time is it?

**MR. HANSON:** It's a quarter after three.

**MRS. HANSON:** That's strange. He comes at three o'clock every day. Where do you think he is? I'm waiting for a very important letter.

**MR. HANSON:** Look, honey. He's coming now.

**MRS. HANSON:** That's not the mail carrier. That's our neighbor Mr. Everet. He's wearing new glasses. Look. He's in his car, but he's not driving away. He's just sitting and reading the newspaper. How strange!

**MR. HANSON:** Is he waiting for his wife?

**MRS. HANSON:** His wife's at work now!

**B. MR. HANSON:** Look! A person on a motorcycle is stopping behind Mr. Everet's car.

**MRS. HANSON:** It's a woman, but it's not Mr. Everet's wife! Who do you think she is?

**MR. HANSON:** I don't know. Look! She's getting off her motorcycle, and she's talking to Mr. Everet.

**MRS. HANSON:** Yes, but he isn't talking. He's just listening.

**MR. HANSON:** Hmm. That's interesting. Look! Now Mr. Everet and the woman are getting on the motorcycle. She's carrying his briefcase, and he's driving! I think this is all very strange. Let's follow those two.

**MRS. HANSON:** Great! Let's get our cameras!

## EXERCISE 2: *Understanding the Conversations*

*Answer the questions in complete sentences.*

1. What do Mr. and Mrs. Hanson do?
2. What are they doing now?
3. What time is it?
4. Who is Mr. Everet?
5. Is Mr. Everet waiting for his wife?

### DISCUSSION

1. Who do you think the woman is?
2. Where do you think she and Mr. Everet are going?
3. Do you think they're spies?

 EXERCISE 3: *What's Happening in the Picture?*

*Write the correct word on the line.*

**behind**
**carrying**
**glasses**
**in front of**
**magazine**
**motorcycle**
**park**
**taking**

1. These people are in the _____ .

2. Mr. and Mrs. Hanson are _____ the car.

3. Mr. Hanson is _____ a picture.

4. The strange woman is _____ a briefcase.

5. She and Mr. Everet are on a _____ .

6. Mr. Everet is _____ the woman.

## VOCABULARY

| | |
|---|---|
| to carry | camera |
| to follow | clock |
| to get | glasses |
| to get on/off | letter |
| to happen | magazine |
| to stop | money |
| to take a picture | motorcycle |
| to think | newspaper |
| to wait (for) | park |
| | story |
| ***Expressions*** | watch |
| How (strange)! | |
| What time is it? | new |
| | strange |
| ***Person/People*** | |
| mail carrier | Which? |
| neighbor | Who? |
| reporter | |
| spy | now |
| | o'clock |
| | |
| | behind |
| | in front of |

## WORD FOR WORD

| What time is it? | | | | |
|---|---|---|---|---|
| It's three o'clock. | It's five after three. | It's a quarter after three. | It's three-thirty. | It's a quarter to three. |
|  |  |  |  |  |

 EXERCISE 4: *What Time Is It?*

*Work with a partner. Look at the clock or watch. Ask the time.*

A: What time is it?
B: It's twenty-five after three.

**1.**

**2.**

**3.**

**4.**

**5.**

**GRAMMAR**

## A. *Present Progressive Tense*

> I **am eating** a hamburger.
> He/She/It **is not eating** a hamburger.
> You/We/They **are eating** hot dogs.

**Spell Check**

drive + ing = driving
ride + ing = riding

sit + ing = sitting
get + ing = getting

 **EXERCISE 5:** *Which Person Is It?*

*Work with a partner. Look at the picture on page 45. Make a sentence about a person. Can your partner guess the person?*

A: This person is standing in front of the bookstore.
B: Is it person H?
A: Yes, it is.

## B. *Present Progressive Tense:* Yes/No Questions and Answers

> John **is running.**
> **Is** he **swimming?**
> Yes, he **is.**/No, **he's not.**/No, he **isn't.**
>
> The girls **are talking.**
> **Are** they **dancing?**
> Yes, they **are.**/No, **they're not.**/No, they **aren't.**

A: Are Mr. and Mrs. Hanson carrying briefcases?
B: No, they aren't. They're carrying cameras.
A: Are they following Mr. Everet?
B: Yes, they are. They think he's a spy.
A: Is he driving his car?
B: No, he isn't. He's riding a motorcycle.
A: How strange!

is + not = isn't
are + not = aren't

 **EXERCISE 6:** *What's the Question?*

*Read the answers. Write **yes/no** questions on the lines.*

1. A: _____
   B: No, Mr. and Mrs. Hanson aren't working today.

2. A: _____
   B: No, they aren't shopping. They're following Mr. Everet.

3. A: _____
   B: Yes, they're taking pictures.

4. A: _____
   B: No, Mr. Everet isn't walking. He's riding a motorcycle.

5. A: _____
   B: Yes, a woman is riding behind him.

## C. *Present Progressive Tense: Information Questions*

> (Mary) **is not shopping.**
> (**What**) **is** (she) **doing?**
> (She) **is riding** her bike.
>
> **Who is** (Mary) **riding** her bike **with?**
> (She) **is riding** her bike **with her sister.**
>
> **Who is riding** the new bike?
> (**Mary's sister**) **is riding** the new bike.

**EXERCISE 7:** *Questions and Answers*

*Read the questions and answers. Write the letter of the correct answer next to the question.*

**1.** What's he doing now? _____
**2.** Where is he riding? _____
**3.** Who is he riding with? _____
**4.** What's she carrying? _____
**5.** Is his wife riding, too? _____

**a.** in the park
**b.** No, she isn't.
**c.** He's riding a motorcycle.
**d.** a briefcase
**e.** a woman

**EXERCISE 8:** *What? Where? Who?*

*Work with a partner. Ask and answer three or four questions about each sentence. Use **what, where,** and **who.***

Barbara is making a pie with her mother at the school.

A: Who is making a pie?
B: Barbara.
A: What's Barbara making?
B: A pie.
A: Who's she making the pie with?
B: Her mother.
A: Where are they making the pie?
B: At the school.

**1.** The reporter is following the spy in the airport.
**2.** The clerks in the hotel are waiting for the woman.
**3.** Steve Maple is writing a new spy story for the magazine.
**4.** My brothers are buying new glasses at the mall.
**5.** The mail carrier is carrying a letter to my neighbor.

## D. *Questions and Sentences with Think*

> **Who do** (you) **think** is going?
> (**I**) **think** the Palmer boys are going.
> **Where do** (you) **think** the boys are going?
> (**I**) **think** they're going to the mall.
> **Do** (you) **think** they're going to the clothes store?
> Yes, (I) **do.**/No, (I) **don't.**

A: Do you think Mr. Everet is a spy?
B: Yes, I do.
A: What do you think he and the woman are doing?
B: I think they're carrying an important letter in that briefcase.
A: Where do you think they're going?
B: I think they're going to the theater.

**EXERCISE 9:** *Scrambled Sentences*

*Write the correct sentence on the line.*

**1.** the   the   you   ?   is   why   spy   think   theater   do   at

_____

**2.** talking   to   .   is   she   actor   an

_____

**3.** too   spy   .   I   think   the   is   actor   a

_____

**4.** is   ?   think   carrying   do   letter   who   the   you

_____

## LISTENING

### *Prelistening*

Look at the pictures. Who are the people? What is happening in each picture?

**EXERCISE 10:**
*What's Happening?*

*Mr. and Mrs. Hanson are watching Mr. Everet and the woman. Listen to the conversation and number the pictures in the correct order.*

## PRONUNCIATION

**EXERCISE 11:** *In /n/, Am /m/, Sing /ŋ/*

Listen to the word. Write an **X** under the word with the same last sound.

| | In | Am | Sing | | In | Am | Sing |
|---|---|---|---|---|---|---|---|
| **1.** | ____ | ____ | ____ | **6.** | ____ | ____ | ____ |
| **2.** | ____ | ____ | ____ | **7.** | ____ | ____ | ____ |
| **3.** | ____ | ____ | ____ | **8.** | ____ | ____ | ____ |
| **4.** | ____ | ____ | ____ | **9.** | ____ | ____ | ____ |
| **5.** | ____ | ____ | ____ | **10.** | ____ | ____ | ____ |

**SPEAKING**

Work with a partner. One partner looks at the picture at the right. The other partner looks at the picture at the bottom of page 52. Find four differences. You can ask only **yes/no** questions.

A: Is a person playing the guitar in your picture?
B: Yes.
A: Is it a boy?
B: No, it's a man.
A: Oh. In my picture, a boy is playing the guitar.

**Picture A**

 **READING**

### Prereading

Mr. Hanson has pictures of Mr. Everet. Mrs. Hanson has pictures of the strange man and woman. Look at the pictures. What's happening?

 **EXERCISE 12:** *What's Happening?*

*Read the sentences. Write the letter of the correct sentence in the box.*

**Mr. Hanson's pictures**

1.

2.

**Mrs. Hanson's pictures**

3.

4.

5.

A. They are talking to a salesperson. The woman is carrying the money from Mr. Everet.

B. The strange man and woman are looking at bikes in a bike store.

C. Mrs. Everet is riding the motorcycle. She likes it. Mr. Everet and their daughter are watching.

D. They are walking out of the store. She has a blue bike, and he has a red bike. They are carrying new backpacks.

E. Mr. Everet and his family are in the park. They are eating a birthday cake. Today is Mrs. Everet's birthday. There is a motorcycle behind the tree. It's for Mrs. Everet.

## EXERCISE 13: *Understanding the Reading*

*Answer the questions.*

1. What is the Everet family doing in the park?
2. What are the strange man and woman doing in the bike store?
3. Who is riding a new motorcycle?

## WRITING

**A. Prewriting. Writing.**
Look at the picture. What's happening? Where are the things and people in the picture? Who are the people? What are they doing? What are they wearing? What color are their clothes? Write eight sentences on a sheet of paper.

**B. Revising. Presenting.** Read your sentences. Is everything correct? Make the corrections. Write the final copy.

## SPEAK OUT!

Work with a partner. Look in a magazine for a picture of men, women, boys and girls. Tell the class about the picture. What is happening? Who are they? Where are they? What are they doing? What time do you think it is?

**Picture B**

# UNIT 7  Let's Get in Shape!

## WARM UP

What kind of exercise do you like to do? How often do you do it? Do you think you are in shape?

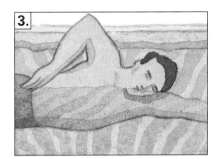

**EXERCISE 1:** *What Can You Do at a Health Club?*

*Look at the pictures. Write the numbers.*

**a.** _____ swim

**b.** _____ run

**c.** _____ lift weights

**d.** _____ exercise

**e.** _____ jump rope

**f.** _____ walk

**g.** _____ ride exercise bikes

**h.** _____ play basketball

**EXERCISE 2:** *Do You Like to Swim?*

*Work with a partner. Look at Exercise 1. What does your partner like to do? Ask and answer questions.*

A: Do you like to swim?
B: No, I don't. Do you like to swim?
A: Yes, I do. I also like to play basketball.
B: Me, too, but I don't like to jump rope.
A: Me, neither.

# DON'T SIT IN FRONT OF YOUR TV!

Exercise and meet new friends at the Fitness Club.
Get in shape now! Come see all the fun!
Come to our Open House tonight at 5:30.

## RUN! Don't Walk!

## CONVERSATIONS

**A. SUE:** Alana, read this ad. The health club wants new members. We can get in shape and meet new friends there.

**ALANA:** I don't need a health club. I'm not out of shape. I exercise every day. I don't have the time or the money to go to a health club.

**SUE:** Oh, come on! There's an Open House tonight. We can have fun there. We can look, and we don't need any money! I know that you're not doing anything tonight.

**ALANA:** OK. You're right. Let's go and see it.

**B. TOM:** Hi, I'm Tom. I work here at the Fitness Club. This is our weight room. Stan and his wife Antonia are lifting weights. They're in great shape. They lift weights every evening. Do you like to lift weights, Sue?

**SUE:** No, I don't. It's very hard.

**TOM:** What kind of exercise do you usually like to do, Alana?

**ALANA:** I like to watch Mel Turner's exercise show on TV. I exercise with him every day. And I like to ride my bike, too. It's fun and easy.

**C. TOM:** Well, this is the big exercise room. There are exercise classes here all day. We have a lot of exercise bikes, too. Some members are riding now. And here is the swimming pool.

**SUE:** Look Alana, there's Julia Bradley. She's swimming in the pool.

**TOM:** Yes, Julia's a new member. A lot of her friends are members of the health club, too. Do you like to play basketball? Julia and her friends play basketball here every week.

**ALANA:** Great! I love to play basketball. What fun!

weight room:

exercise bike:

**D.** **TOM:** Here's the health food bar. You can have breakfast, lunch, dinner, or a snack here. You can see that a lot of members are sitting at the bar now.

**SUE:** Hey, isn't that Ted Crampton?

**TED:** Hi! Don't you think the health club is great? Do you want a drink? They have juice—orange, apple, or grape—and water, of course.

**SUE:** Yes, I'd like some apple juice. Thank you. How often do you come to the health club, Ted?

**TED:** Oh, I come every day! I like the Fitness Club.

**SUE:** Me, too! What do you think, Alana?

**ALANA:** Good-by TV and hello Fitness Club!!

**health food bar:**

---

**EXERCISE 3:** *Understanding the Conversations*

*Answer the questions.*

**1.** What kind of exercise does Alana like?
**2.** Who do Alana and Sue know at the Fitness Club?
**3.** What can you do at the Fitness Club?

---

**EXERCISE 4:** *Do You Know How to Swim?*

**A.** *Write three things you know how to do and three things you don't know how to do on a sheet of paper.*

**B.** *Choose something you don't know how to do. Find someone who can teach you how to do it. Then find someone you can teach how to do something.*

A: Do you know how to swim?
B: Yes, I do.
A: I don't know how to swim, but I want to learn. Can you teach me?
B: Of course. No problem.

---

**EXERCISE 5:** *Food and Drinks*

*What food do you eat at breakfast, lunch, and dinner? What do you have as a snack? Do you eat healthy food?*

Breakfast _____

Lunch _____

Dinner _____

Snack _____

**WORD FOR WORD**

*Have*

**Have** means "possession."
Use the simple present
tense of **have**.

> I **have** a new car.
> I **don't have** time to talk with you.
> I **don't have** the money to go.

**Have** can also be used in
expressions. Then you can
use the simple present or the
present progressive tense
of **have**.

> I'm **having** a good time. I **have** a good time at the health
>   club every evening.
> We're **not having** fun. We **don't have** fun at work.
> He's **having** a hot dog and milk for lunch. He **has** a hot
> dog and milk for lunch every day.

 **EXERCISE 6:** *Have a Try!*

*Work with a partner. Ask and answer the questions. Think of
the way you use* ***have.***

**1.** Do you have a large family? How many brothers and sisters
   do you have?
**2.** What do you like to have for lunch? for breakfast? for
   dinner?
**3.** Are you having fun in class today?

**G** **GRAMMAR**

**A.** *Simple Present
Tense with Every*

> How often do Mr. and Mrs. Barrett swim?
> They swim **every** morning.
>        **every** Sunday.
>        **every** Friday afternoon.

 **EXERCISE 7:** *Talk About Your Life*

**A.** *Write five sentences about yourself on a sheet of paper.*

I go to English class every day.

**1.** every morning     **3.** every week     **5.** every year
**2.** every afternoon     **4.** every day

**B.** *Work with a partner. Find out what your partner does. Ask
and answer questions.*

A: What do you do every morning?
B: I eat a large breakfast. What do you do?
A: I ride my exercise bike.

## B. *Simple Present Tense vs. Present Progressive Tense*

Use the simple present tense to talk about things that happen a lot.

> What **do** you **do** on Saturday morning?
> I **ride** my bike.
> Do you **ride** your bike every Saturday?
> Yes, I **do.**

Use the present progressive tense to talk about things that are happening now.

> What **is** Liz **doing** now?
> She**'s riding** her bike.
> **Is** she **riding** in the park?
> Yes, she **is.**

| **A lot** | **Now** |
|---|---|
| in the afternoon | this afternoon |
| on Saturday | today |
| every week | now |

**EXERCISE 8:** *Yoko's Afternoon Schedule*

**A.** *Look at Yoko's schedule. Work with a partner. Ask and answer the questions.*

| Yoko's Afternoon Schedule | | | | | | |
|---|---|---|---|---|---|---|
| SUN | MON | TUES | WED | THURS | FRI | SAT |
| read | do English homework | swim | work in father's office | do English homework | bake a cake | go to the park with friends |

**1.** What does Yoko do every Friday afternoon?
**2.** When does Yoko do her English homework?
**3.** Where does Yoko work every Wednesday afternoon?
**4.** What does Yoko do every Sunday afternoon?
**5.** When does Yoko swim?
**6.** What do Yoko and her friends do every Saturday afternoon?

**B.** *Work with a partner. Ask and answer the questions.*

**1.** It's Tuesday afternoon. What is Yoko doing?
**2.** Yoko is baking a cake now. What day is it?
**3.** It's Monday afternoon. What is Yoko doing?
**4.** It's Sunday afternoon. What is Yoko doing?
**5.** Yoko is working in her father's office now. What day is it?

## C. *Imperatives*

> In the exercise class:
> **Run. Walk. Don't Stop.**
>
> In the classroom:
> **Listen.** Please **sit down. Repeat.**
> **Don't talk,** please. **Raise** your hands.
> **Close** your books, please.

**EXERCISE 9:** *Who Says What?*

*Work with a partner. Who is talking? Who are they talking to? Several answers are possible.*

| a mother | a father |
|---|---|
| a husband | a musician |
| a spy | a doctor |
| a clerk | a wife |
| a teacher | a student |
| a friend | a child |

1. Eat a lot of fruit.
2. Eat your food!
3. Don't buy a cake.
4. Exercise every day.
5. Write your answers on a sheet of paper.
6. Fill in the form, please.
7. Don't play my guitar!
8. Don't wear that short skirt.
9. Have a good vacation.
10. Follow that man!

## LISTENING

### Prelistening

Look at the pictures. Where are these people? What do you think they are doing?

**EXERCISE 10:**

*The New Health Club Member*

*Listen to the conversation. What are the office workers doing now? Write each name under the correct picture.*

| Richard | Luis | Tony |
|---|---|---|
| Sandra | Mona | Brian |
| Harold | | |

1. _____, _____

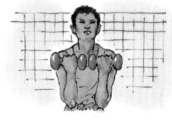

4. _____

2. _____, _____

5. _____

3. _____

## PRONUNCIATION

**EXERCISE 11:** *Like /l/, Right /r/, Window /w/*

*Listen and repeat. Listen for the beginning sound in **like**, in **right**, and in **window**.*

| Like | Right | Window | Like | Right | Window |
|---|---|---|---|---|---|
| let's | raise | word | eleven | address | between |
| lettuce | read | wife | hello | across | twenty |
| like | red | white | milk | briefcase | sandwich |

**EXERCISE 12:** *Like /l/ Right /r/ or Window /w/?*

*Listen to each word. Circle **l**
if you hear the same beginning
sound as in **like**. Circle **r** if
you hear the same beginning
sound as in **right**. Circle **w** if
you hear the same beginning
sound as in **window**.*

| | | | | | | | |
|---|---|---|---|---|---|---|---|
| **1.** | l | r | w | **6.** | l | r | w |
| **2.** | l | r | w | **7.** | l | r | w |
| **3.** | l | r | w | **8.** | l | r | w |
| **4.** | l | r | w | **9.** | l | r | w |
| **5.** | l | r | w | **10.** | l | r | w |

# SPEAKING

**A.** You are a reporter. You are
writing about health for your
newspaper. You want to talk
to some people about their
ideas. Work with a partner.
Find out what he or she thinks
about his or her health. Here
are some questions you can
ask. Think of your own
questions, too.

**B.** Tell the class about your
partner.

Do you exercise?
Do you like to exercise?
What kind of exercise do you like to do?
How often do you exercise?
Where do you like to exercise?
Do you like to eat healthy food?
What food do you like to eat?
Do you like to eat a snack between meals? Is this healthy?
What drinks do you like?
Do you read books about health?
Do you watch TV shows about health or exercise?
Do you walk to school or to work?
Do you think you're healthy?
Do you think you're in shape?

# READING

## Prereading

**A.** Are you in shape? What
do you do to get in shape?
Do you have a lot of time to
exercise? Does your school
have a health program for
its students? Do you know
any offices that have exercise
rooms for the workers?

**B.** Look at the pictures.
Where are the people? What
are they doing? Read the title
on page 60. What do you
think **working out** means?
What do you think the
reading is about?

---

**Working Out At Work**

A lot of people are out of shape. They say that they don't have time to exercise or to eat right. For this reason, many companies are now providing exercise centers and health classes for their workers.

5     Workers in both large and small companies can exercise during their lunch hour. For example, at Texas Instruments, Inc., in Dallas, there is an exercise center with fitness instructors and nutrition classes for the 22,000 employees. At one of Nike's locations, there is a weight machine, two

10  exercise bicycles, and two rowing machines for the 300 employees. British Rail at Waterloo Station in London has an exercise room for its employees.

     At Bonne Bell in Ohio, employees get thirty extra minutes at lunchtime if they want to exercise. And they can wear

15  exercise clothes at work in the afternoon. If a Bonne Bell employee exercises four days a week for half a year, he or she gets $250 from the company!

     It is important to be healthy and in shape. But don't wait for your company or school to start a health program. You can

20  eat right and start your own exercise routine right now.

**company:** place you work

**provide:** have

**fitness:** health

**nutrition:** healthy eating

**employee:** worker

**rowing machine:**

**extra:** +

**half:** 1/2

 **EXERCISE 13:** *Understanding the Reading*

*Read the sentence. Circle **T** for true and **F** for false. Explain your answers.*

**1.**  T  F   Both large and small companies have health programs for their workers.
**2.**  T  F   Nike employees can get money if they exercise a lot.
**3.**  T  F   Employees can go to classes on healthy eating at Texas Instruments, Inc.
**4.**  T  F   You need to wait for your company or school to start a health program.

 **WRITING**

**A. Prewriting. Writing.** You are writing a list of ideas for good health. Work with a partner. Write fifteen ideas. Choose ten ideas you like best and write them on a sheet of paper. Write complete sentences.

**B. Revising. Presenting.** Read the sentences. Is everything correct? Make the corrections. Write the final copy. Tell the class your ideas.

**DISCUSSION**

1. Do you think health programs for students and workers are good? Explain.

2. Can you be healthy but not exercise? Can you exercise but not be healthy? Explain.

**SPEAK OUT!**

You and your partner work at a health club. You want new members. Make a TV ad about your club. Then present your ad to the class. (Name your health club. Talk about what you can do there. Tell the hours the club is open. Tell the cost of membership. Tell where the club is.)

# UNIT 8 Soap Suds

## WARM UP

What are they doing? How
do they feel?

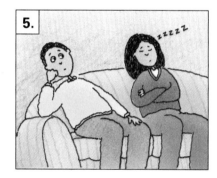

**EXERCISE 1: *How Do They Feel?***

**A.** *Look at the pictures. Match each picture with the correct word.*

| | | | |
|---|---|---|---|
| 1. _____ | 5. _____ | **a.** angry | **e.** nervous |
| 2. _____ | 6. _____ | **b.** sad | **f.** happy |
| 3. _____ | 7. _____ | **c.** sick | **g.** shocked |
| 4. _____ | 8. _____ | **d.** worried | **h.** tired |

**B.** *Look at the pictures. Work with a partner. Ask and answer questions.*

A: What's she doing?
B: She's eating some cake.
A: How does she feel?
B: She feels happy.

**CONVERSATIONS**

In the last *Soap Suds* magazine, David and Mona were in love. But today something happened. . . .

### SCENE 1

Mona, darling! I can't live without you!

Oh, David, my good friend . . .

### SCENE 2

What are you saying? Why did you call me "friend"? I'm your boyfriend. I love you.

I'm sorry, David. Don't be angry with me, but I don't love you.

### SCENE 3

Angry? I'm sad, very sad—and shocked. Mona, I don't understand. Just yesterday we danced to our favorite music!

Yes, we did. But I don't love you today. I'm returning your ring.

### SCENE 4

Stop, listen to me. . . Mona, is there another man?

I'm sorry David, but there is. I love him now and not you.

### SCENE 5

I knew it! But I'm so confused. We were in love. And now you love another man, and I'm alone. I can't stand it! Good-by, Mona.

Oh, David wait! Can't we be friends?

**EXERCISE 2:**
*Understanding the Conversations*

*Answer the questions.*

1. Does David love Mona?
2. Did Mona love David yesterday?
3. Does Mona love David now?
4. Why is David confused?
5. Do you think Mona and David can be friends?

**EXERCISE 3:** *Vocabulary Check*

**A.** *Work with a partner. Ask and answer the questions. Use these words. You can answer with more than one word.*

| | | | | |
|---|---|---|---|---|
| afraid | great | hungry | shocked | thirsty |
| angry | happy | nervous | sick | tired |
| confused | healthy | sad | terrible | worried |

**1.** You get a thousand dollars from your friend. How do you feel?
**2.** You have a test now. How do you feel?
**3.** You lifted weights for fifty minutes. How do you feel?
**4.** You're flying a plane for the first time. How do you feel?
**5.** You want to eat. How do you feel?
**6.** Your family buys a new house. How do you feel?
**7.** The baby is crying. How do you feel?

**B.** *Think of more examples and ask another student questions.*

## WORD FOR WORD

### *Adverbs of Time*

| Then | Now |
|---|---|
| yesterday | today |
| yesterday morning | this morning |
| yesterday afternoon | this afternoon |
| yesterday evening | this evening |
| last night | tonight |
| last week | this week |
| last Thursday | Thursday |
| last year | this year |
| last month | this month |

# Vocabulary

| to be: was/were | **Pronouns** | **Feelings** |
|---|---|---|
| to call | him | afraid |
| to cry | me | angry |
| to laugh | them | confused |
| to love | us | happy |
| to return | | nervous |
| to say | home | sad |
| to smile | homework | shocked |
| | hour | sick |
| alone | house | terrible |
| favorite | minute | worried |
| in love | ring | |
| | soap opera | because |
| **Expressions** | yesterday | |
| How do you feel? | | How long? |
| I can't stand it! | | Why? |

**EXERCISE 4:** *What Did You Do?*

*Work with a partner. What did you do? What did your partner do? Write the verb on the line. Then tell the class.*

| What did you do . . . ? | I . . . . | My partner . . . . |
|---|---|---|
| **1.** last night | _____ | _____ |
| **2.** last Monday | _____ | _____ |
| **3.** yesterday afternoon | _____ | _____ |
| **4.** last year | _____ | _____ |
| **5.** last week | _____ | _____ |

**GRAMMAR**

## A. *The Simple Past Tense:*
## *Yes/No Questions and Short Answers with To Be*

I/He/She/It **was** not sad.
**Was** (he) angry?
Yes, (he) **was**./No, (he) **wasn't**.

You/We/They **were not** at the mall.
**Were** (they) at the park?
Yes, (they) **were**./No, (they) **weren't**.

 **EXERCISE 5:** *Was Your Sister Angry?*

*Ask and answer questions.*

**your sister/angry**
A: Was your sister angry yesterday?
B: Yes, she was.

**Joe and Sue/in the park**
A: Were Joe and Sue in the park yesterday afternoon?
B: No, they weren't. They were at the health club.

| *Use These Words* |
| --- |
| yesterday |
| yesterday morning/afternoon/evening |
| last night/week/year/Thursday |

1. you/nervous
2. your teacher/sick
3. your friend/at school
4. your mother and father/at the theater
5. your books/on the desk
6. your daughter/happy

## B. *The Simple Past Tense:*
## *Information Questions with To Be*

**Who was** angry?
(The boyfriend) **was** angry.
How long **was** (he) angry?
(He) **was** angry for two hours.

**Who was** confused?
(The students) **were** confused.
**(Why) were** (they) confused.
Because (they) **were** nervous.

 **EXERCISE 6:** *What's the Question?*

*Write the correct question for each answer.*

1. (*Where?*) _____ He was at the mall last night.

2. (*Yes/No?*) _____ No, he wasn't alone.

3. (*Who?*) _____ He was with his wife.

4. (*How long?*) _____ They were at the mall for three hours.

5. (*Yes/No?*) _____ Yes, they were in Style City.

6. (*Why?*) _____ Because they returned a shirt.

## C. *The Simple Past Tense:*
## *Yes/No Questions and Short Answers*

> I/You/He/She/We/They **lifted** weights.
> **Did** (he) **jump** rope?
> Yes, (he) **did.**/No, (he) **didn't.**

 **EXERCISE 7:** *Did You Talk to Your Mother Yesterday?*

*Write questions about yesterday on a sheet of paper. Use these verbs. Then ask another student your questions.*

| | |
|---|---|
| talk | Did you talk to your mother yesterday? Yes, I did. |
| walk | Did you walk in the park yesterday?<br>No, I didn't. I was at home all day. |

**1.** listen to  **3.** study  **5.** cook  **7.** call
**2.** work  **4.** exercise  **6.** dance  **8.** play

## D. *The Simple Past Tense: Information Questions*

| | |
|---|---|
| **What did** you **do** yesterday? | I **watched** a soap opera. |
| **Where did** you **watch** it? | At home. |
| **Who did** you **watch** it with? | With my mother. |
| **How long did** you **watch** it? | We **watched** it for one hour. |
| **When did** you **call** Mona? | At eight o'clock. |
| **Why did** you **call** her? | **Because** I **needed** to talk to her. |

**EXERCISE 8:** *Mona and David*

*Fill in the correct verbs. Use these words. You can use the words more than one time.*

| did | |
|---|---|
| **didn't** | FRAN: Mona, what **(1)** _____ David **(2)** _____ last Sunday night? |
| **play** | MONA: He **(3)** _____ English at his house. |
| **played** | FRAN: **(4)** _____ you **(5)** _____ with him? |
| **do** | MONA: No, I **(6)** _____ . |
| **study** | FRAN: What did you **(7)** _____ ? |
| **studied** | MONA: I **(8)** _____ basketball. |

## E. *Object Pronouns*

Use object prepositions after verbs and prepositions.

| I | **me** | we | **us** |
|---|---|---|---|
| he | **him** | you | **you** |
| she | **her** | they | **them** |
| it | **it** | | |

| |
|---|
| He loves **me.** |
| He's angry with **me.** |

**EXERCISE 9:** *Write the Word!*

Write the correct pronoun on the line.

My husband Tony loves the theater. I go with **(1)** _____ every Friday night. Sometimes
our daughter and son go with **(2)** _____ to the theater. Sometimes I talk in the theater. My
family gets angry with **(3)** _____ and says, "Be quiet. We're listening to the actors, not to
**(4)** _____ ." But I'm not angry with **(5)** _____ because they're my family.

Then we usually go to our favorite place to eat, Pasta Pronto. We like **(6)** _____ a lot.
Everyone there knows **(7)** _____ and says hello. They like our daughter a lot, and
they always smile at **(8)** _____ .

# LISTENING

## *Prelistening*

Do you watch soap operas on TV? Do you listen to soap
operas on the radio? In the United States in the 1940s and
1950s, there were a lot of soap operas on the radio. Are there
radio soap operas in your country? What are their names?

**EXERCISE 10:** *The World Is Small, A Radio Soap Opera*

*Read the questions. Listen to the soap opera. Circle the best
answer to each question.*

**1.** What is wrong with Maria?
   **a.** Maria thinks Roberto loves another woman.
   **b.** Maria thinks Antonio doesn't love her.
   **c.** Maria thinks she doesn't love Antonio or Roberto.

**2.** Why didn't Maria talk to Roberto in the park?
   **a.** Antonio was with her.
   **b.** She was angry and confused.
   **c.** She didn't like him.

**3.** How does Maria feel?
   **a.** She feels afraid and confused.
   **b.** She feels alone, but happy.
   **c.** She feels confused and sad.

# PRONUNCIATION

**EXERCISE 11:** *Is It Past Tense?*

*Listen to the verbs. Do you
hear a past tense ending?
Circle the word you hear.*

| | | | | |
|---|---|---|---|---|
| **1.** play | played | | **4.** stop | stopped |
| **2.** dance | danced | | **5.** need | needed |
| **3.** wait | waited | | **6.** exercise | exercised |

**SPEAKING**

Work with a group of people. You are one of the people in
a soap opera. Each person in the soap opera has a feeling.
Ask each other questions about your feelings. Why does each
person feel that way? Make up a story. Then share your ideas
with the class.

| Useful Language |
| --- |
| How do you feel? |
| I feel (angry). |
| Why do you feel (angry)? |
| I feel (angry) because . . . |

 **READING**

### Prereading

Do you read magazines or newspapers about soap operas? Do
you know anyone who reads them? What's in them? Look at
the page. What soap opera is the page about?

## WHAT HAPPENED IN THE SOAPS LAST WEEK?

### Family Trees

MONDAY

Susan didn't work for ten years. Then she wanted to start teaching
again. But she thought that Frank, her husband, didn't want her to work.
Susan was very sad and confused. She didn't know what to do.

Susan called her friend Angela. She talked to her about her problem.
Angela said, "Follow your heart. You love to teach. Talk to Frank."

Billy, Susan's son, asked a new girlfriend to go to the mall with
him.

TUESDAY

Billy is having problems in school. Billy's teacher called Susan and
said that he didn't study, listen, or do his homework. Susan cried. She
was very worried. Susan talked to Billy about school, but he didn't want
to talk about it. All he wanted to do was be with his new girlfriend.

Susan waited for Frank to come home. She wanted to talk to him
about their son. Frank didn't come home until ten o'clock. Susan was in
bed. She didn't talk to him about anything.

WEDNESDAY

Susan talked to Frank in the morning. He called Billy's teacher. At
work, Frank asked some men about their wives. A lot of wives worked.
He was confused. Their family needed money, but he wanted Susan to
be at home. And now Billy needs help.

Susan looked in the newspaper for a job. Billy went to the mall
again with his new girlfriend. He didn't study for his test.

**again:** another time

**said:** *say* in the past tense

**help:** to do something that is needed

---

**EXERCISE 12:** *Understanding the Reading*

*Read the sentence. Circle **T** for **true** and **F** for **false**. Explain.*

1. T  F  Susan works at a school.
2. T  F  Angela is Billy's girlfriend.
3. T  F  Susan is worried about her son.
4. T  F  Frank doesn't want Susan to work.
5. T  F  Susan's family needs money.

## WRITING

**A. Prewriting. Writing.**
You are a writer for *Soap Summaries*. Look at the pictures. What happened in *Family Trees* on Thursday and on Friday? Write a paragraph about the soap opera using the pictures.

**B. Revising. Presenting.** Read the paragraph. Is everything correct? Make any corrections. Write the final copy.

THURSDAY

FRIDAY

## SPEAK OUT!

Work with a partner. Choose a favorite soap opera or other TV program. Did you watch the show last week? Talk about two people from the show. What happened to them last week? Tell the class.

# UNIT 9 Interesting People and Places

## WARM UP

**A.** What do you like to do on vacation? Do you like to discover new things? go to interesting places? eat new foods? learn about famous people?

**B.** Miriam is going on vacation in Mexico. What does she want to do?

**1.** eat in restaurants

**4.** climb a mountain

**7.** go to famous places

**2.** ride a bike

**5.** see pyramids

**8.** take a lot of pictures

**3.** swim

**6.** speak Spanish

**9.** write post cards

 EXERCISE 1: *What Did Miriam Do on Vacation?*

*Miriam got back from her vacation yesterday. What did she do? Work with a partner. Ask and answer questions.*

**1.** ate
A: Where did Miriam eat?
B: She ate in some good restaurants.

**2.** rode
**3.** swam
**4.** climbed

**5.** saw
**6.** spoke
**7.** went to

**8.** took
**9.** wrote

---

UNIT 9  INTERESTING PEOPLE AND PLACES

69

## CONVERSATIONS

**A.** **JOHN:** We need to remember a lot for our ancient history test. Why don't you ask me some questions first? Then I can ask you some questions.

**MARK:** Fine. Let's see . . . first question. Who wrote *The Iliad*?

**JOHN:** That's easy. Homer wrote *The Iliad*.

**MARK:** Second question. What was *The Iliad* about?

**JOHN:** It was about a war between Greece and Troy.

**MARK:** Was it about a real war?

**JOHN:** Yes, it was. For a long time people thought the war didn't really happen. They thought *The Iliad* was just a story. But Heinrich Schliemann read it, and he thought it was true. He looked for the ruins of Troy, and he found them in the 1870s.

**MARK:** Did the Trojans win the war?

**JOHN:** No, they didn't. They lost.

**ancient:** very old

**Troy:**

**Trojans:** people from Troy

**B.** **JOHN:** OK. Now I want to ask some questions. Who built Stonehenge and when?

**MARK:** Ancient people of England built it in about 1800 B.C. We don't really know who they were or how they did it. But we know what they did there.

**JOHN:** What did they do at Stonehenge?

**MARK:** They watched the sun, the moon, and the stars, and they made a calendar.

**Stonehenge:**

**C.** **JOHN:** All right. Here are the last questions. Where are the ruins of the famous Mayan city of Tikal?

**MARK:** Oh, that's easy. They're in Guatemala.

**JOHN:** When did the Mayas live there?

**MARK:** They started to build stone buildings there in about 900 B.C. They lived there to about A.D. 900.

**JOHN:** Great! I think we're ready for our test.

**Tikal:**

*These questions were on John and Mark's history test. Circle the correct answers.*

1. What was *The Iliad* about?
   a. a real war
   b. a war that never happened
   c. Heinrich Schliemann's discoveries

2. Who won the Trojan War?
   a. the Trojans
   b. the Greeks
   c. No one. It never happened.

3. Who discovered the ruins of Troy?
   a. Homer
   b. the ancient Greeks
   c. Heinrich Schliemann

4. Where is Stonehenge?
   a. Greece
   b. England
   c. Guatemala

5. Where is Tikal?
   a. Greece
   b. England
   c. Guatemala

6. Who built Tikal?
   a. the Greeks
   b. the Trojans
   c. the Mayas

📝 EXERCISE 3: *Vocabulary Check*

*Write the letter of the correct picture on the line.*

1. post card _____
2. mountain _____
3. calendar _____
4. moon _____
5. star _____
6. sun _____
7. building _____
8. ruins _____

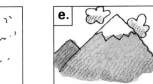

## VOCABULARY

| New Past Tense Forms | |
| --- | --- |
| buy/bought | building |
| come/came | calendar |
| do/did | date |
| eat/ate | history |
| get/got back | moon |
| go/went | mountain |
| have/had | post card |
| make/made | ruins |
| read/read | star |
| ride/rode | stone |
| see/saw | sun |
| speak/spoke | test |
| swim/swam | war |
| take/took | |
| think/thought | beautiful |
| write/wrote | famous |
| | real |
| | second |
| | third |

**Regular Verbs**
climb
discover
learn
look for
remember

**Irregular Verbs**
build/built
find/found
lose/lost
win/won

**Expressions**
Why don't you (start)?
When (were) (you) born?

📝 EXERCISE 4: *Same or Opposite?*

*Do these words mean the same or the opposite? Write **S** (same) or **O** (opposite) on the line.*

_____ 1. went      came
_____ 2. found    discovered
_____ 3. built      made

_____ 4. answered    asked
_____ 5. looked at    saw
_____ 6. won          lost

# WORD FOR WORD

## A. Ordinal Numbers

Cardinal numbers tell how many.
Ordinal numbers tell what's next.

> The building has **thirteen** floors.
> Joe lives on the **thirteenth** floor.

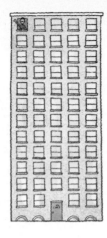

thirteenth (13th)
twelfth (12th)
eleventh (11th)
tenth (10th)
ninth (9th)
eighth (8th)
seventh (7th)
sixth (6th)
fifth (5th)
fourth (4th)
third (3rd)
second (2nd)
first (1st)

## B. Dates

> When were you born? I was born on **September fourteenth, 1976.**
> When is your mother's birthday? Her birthday is **July 7th.**

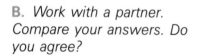

## EXERCISE 5: Birthdays

**A.** When do you think these famous people were born?

**a.** July 24, 1783
**b.** November 19, 1917
**c.** July 12, 100 B.C.
**d.** March 12, 1879

**B.** Work with a partner. Compare your answers. Do you agree?

A: When do you think Albert Einstein was born?
B: I think he was born on March twelfth, eighteen seventy-nine.

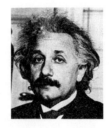

**1.** Albert Einstein

**2.** Simón Bolívar

**3.** Indira Gandhi

**4.** Julius Caesar

# GRAMMAR

## The Simple Past Tense: Irregular Verbs

The past tense of many English verbs is not spelled with **-ed.**

| Regular Verbs | Irregular Verbs |
|---|---|
| (Luis) **studied** last night. | (Carol) **bought** a TV last week. |
| **Did** (he) **study** with Mark? | **Did** (she) **buy** it at the mall? |
| Yes, (he) **did.**/No, (he) **didn't.** | Yes, (she) **did.**/No, (she) **didn't.** |
| **(Where) did** they study? | **(Why) did** she **buy** a TV? |
| They **studied** at Mark's house. | Because she **didn't have** a TV. |

## EXERCISE 6: *Verb Forms*

*Circle the answers.*

**1.** In questions use:          **eat    ate    study    studied.**
**2.** In sentences with **not** use:   **eat    ate    study    studied.**
**3.** In sentences without **not** use:  **eat    ate    study    studied.**

## EXERCISE 7: *What Did You Do Last Week?*

**A.** *What did you do last week? Write* **yes** *or* **no** *under* **You.**

**B.** *Work with a partner. Ask questions. Write* **yes** *or* **no** *under* **Your partner.**

A: Did you buy any new clothes last week?
B: No, I didn't. Did you buy any new clothes last week?
A: Yes, I did.

|  | You | Your Partner |
|---|---|---|
| **1.** bought some new clothes | _____ | _____ |
| **2.** cooked dinner | _____ | _____ |
| **3.** had a test | _____ | _____ |
| **4.** listened to music | _____ | _____ |
| **5.** rode a bike | _____ | _____ |
| **6.** studied English | _____ | _____ |
| **7.** swam | _____ | _____ |
| **8.** went to a mall | _____ | _____ |

## EXERCISE 8: *What Did Tom Do Last Week?*

*Work with a partner. What did Tom do last week? Ask and answer questions. One partner looks at Calendar A. The other partner looks at Calendar B on page 76. Fill in Tom's calendar.*

A: What did Tom do on Monday?
B: He bought new pants.

**Calendar A**

| | |
|---|---|
| MON. | _____ |
| TUES. | got an interesting post card from a friend |
| WED. | _____ |
| THURS. | spoke with his teacher about the test |
| FRI. | _____ |
| SAT. | looked for a new jacket at the mall |
| SUN. | _____ |

## LISTENING

### Prelistening

**A.** What interesting places do you know about? Where did you learn about them?

**B.** Do you know these places? What do you know about them?

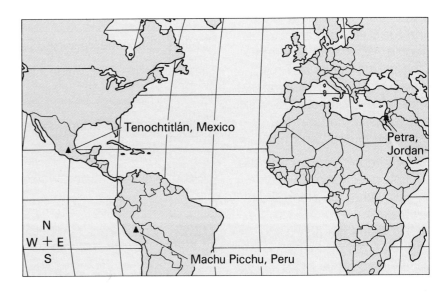

Tenochtitlán, Mexico

Petra, Jordan

N
W + E
S

Machu Picchu, Peru

### EXERCISE 9: *What Did You Learn?*

Listen to the conversation. What did the students learn about these people? Write an **X**.

1. had houses with one room

2. had buildings of red stone

3. had buildings of white stone

4. wrote with pictures

5. lived in the mountains

|  | Nabateans | Incas | Aztecs |
|---|---|---|---|
|  |  |  |  |
|  |  |  |  |
|  |  |  |  |
|  |  |  |  |
|  |  |  |  |

## PRONUNCIATION

### EXERCISE 10: *Think /θ/*

*Listen and repeat.*

1. thanks
2. third
3. Thursday
4. three
5. thought
6. birthday
7. healthy
8. month
9. thirteenth
10. twentieth

### EXERCISE 11: *Do You Hear It?*

*Listen to the words. Some have the same beginning sound as **think** and others don't. Write **yes** when you hear the beginning sound of **think** and **no** when you don't.*

1. _____
2. _____
3. _____
4. _____
5. _____
6. _____
7. _____
8. _____

## SPEAKING

You need to complete a time line for a test on famous people. Work with a partner. One partner looks at Time Line A. The other looks at Time Line B on page 76. Ask questions to find out the information you don't have.

A: Why don't you ask me the first question?

B: OK. What did Henry Ford make?

A: He made his first car.

B: When did he make it?

A: He made it in 1893.

| Time Line A | |
|---|---|
| 1600 | Shakespeare wrote _____ . |
| 1893 | Henry Ford made his first car. |
|  |  _____ found ruins on Crete, Greece. |
| 1926 | Gertrude Ederle swam the English Channel. |
|  | Walt Disney _____ . |
| 1969 | Neil Armstrong walked on the moon. |
|  | Mark Spitz won _____ . |
| 1975 | Mrs. Junko Tabei climbed Mount Everest. |

 **READING**

## *Prereading*

Look at the picture. Do you know about this place? Where is it?

### Hiram Bingham and the Lost City of Machu Picchu

Hiram Bingham (1875–1956) was a history teacher. He wanted to learn about the ancient people of South America. He visited South America five times and discovered many ancient ruins. His most famous discovery was in Peru. It was
5 the ruins of Machu Picchu, the lost city of the Incas.

The Incas lived in South America for three hundred years. Then, in the 1500s, they lost a war with the Spanish. The Spanish tried to destroy everything that the Incas built, but people said there was still an old city somewhere in the
10 mountains.

**destroy:** make into ruins

**still:** at that time

Many people searched for Machu Picchu, but no one found it. Then, in 1911, Bingham learned about some ruins on a mountain next to the Urubamba River. Bingham climbed the mountain, and there was the city!

15 At one time, a thousand people lived in Machu Picchu. They built long streets and beautiful stone buildings. One building was an observatory where they watched the sun, moon, and stars. They told time by the stars and made a calendar to mark the hours, days, and years.

**told time:** learned what time

20 When did these people leave Machu Picchu? Where did they go? No one knows.

Today tourists can take buses up to these famous ruins. They walk on the streets and take pictures of the houses. They like being in this ancient place.

### EXERCISE 12: *Getting Meaning from Context*

*Find the word in the the reading. Circle the answer that means the same.*

| | | | |
|---|---|---|---|
| **1.** visited (*line 3*) | **a.** read about | **b.** looked for | **c.** went to |
| **2.** lost (*line 5*) | **a.** not won | **b.** not found | **c.** old |
| **3.** searched for (*line 11*) | **a.** talked about | **b.** saw | **c.** looked for |
| **4.** tourists (*line 22*) | **a.** people on business | **b.** people on vacation | **c.** bus drivers |
| **5.** up (*line 22*) | **a.** ↓ | **b.** ↑ | **c.** ← |

# UNIT *10* *What's Your Opinion?*

## WARM UP

**A.** There are a lot of ads in newspapers, in magazines, and on TV. Do you read or listen to the ads? What kinds of information do you find in ads?

**B.** Read these ads. Do they answer questions with **who, what, when,** and **where?**

---

Do you want a good job? Study at Robert's Secretarial School. We can teach you to type in one day! Don't wait! Call for an interview any day before 9 P.M. We're at 1946 Park Street. Our telephone number is (708) 375-0700.

---

Cooper's Baby Food on sale today at City Market, 927 Green Street. Open every day from 7 A.M. to 10 P.M.
Phone (708) 375-8976.

---

**Are you tall?**
Do you need to wear big clothes? Come to Highland's Big and Tall Men's Store. SALE THIS WEEKEND on all pants!
250 Mountain View Road
**(815) 354-6057**

---

Do you want to get in shape and be thin? Come to **L.A. Health Club.** Say good-by to your fat! We have early morning classes. Come in for one free class!
ADDRESS: 1410 Lake Avenue
PHONE: (708) 375-0909

---

Shoe City is having a sale! Saturday 10 A.M. to 10:00 P.M. Come early or late, but come!
165 Green Street
**(815) 354-6677**

---

**DERMIT'S LANGUAGE SCHOOL**
We can teach you to speak Spanish, French, Italian, German, Russian, Arabic, or Japanese. We have classes for adults and children. We have classes in the morning, afternoon, and evening, and on the weekend.
**CALL TODAY.**
Our phone number is (708) 375-7676.
Or come to our office at 675 Park Street.

---

Do you need someone to clean your house? CALL MRS. CLEAN. Our people can clean anything, and they can come anytime. Call us today at (815) 354-2441 and have a clean house tonight!
367 MOUNTAIN VIEW ROAD

---

We want you to be our reporters! Tell us what's happening in the city. Call us at (708) 375-7575 with your news. We're here every day, 24 hours a day.
**WNTC Radio** **1232 Lake Avenue**

---

 **EXERCISE 1:** *What? When? Where?*

*Look at the ads. Work with a partner. Ask and answer questions about them with* ***what, when,*** *and* ***where.***

A: What does Robert's Secretarial School teach you to do?
B: Type.
A: When can I call?
B: Every day before nine P.M.
A: Where is the school?
B: It's on Park Street.

---

**EXERCISE 2: *Where Can You Go? Who Can You Call?***

*Answer the questions about the ads on page 77.*

**1.** Your father is very tall. You want to buy some pants for his birthday. Where can you go?
**2.** Your mother wants you to buy some food for the baby. Where can you go?
**3.** You want your son to learn Italian. Where can he go?
**4.** Your house is dirty. You don't have time to clean it. You want someone to clean it for you. Who can you call?
**5.** You want to teach people to be healthy. Where can you look for a job?
**6.** You and your friends saw a famous actor at the airport. You think this is interesting news. Who can you call?

## CONVERSATIONS

**A. REPORTER:** Good afternoon. I'm Doug Lee. Welcome to *Person on the Street.* Every week I ask people questions. I find out their opinions about something in the news. Excuse me, ma'am. I'd like to ask you a question.

**WOMAN 1:** All right. What is it?

**REPORTER:** The city wants to build a new office building next to the park. What do you think about it?

**WOMAN 1:** Oh, I saw the design for that on TV. It's a tall, ugly building. I don't want the city to build it.

**REPORTER:** How about you, sir? What do you think?

**MAN 1:** I agree with her. I don't want them to build it next to our pretty park. They're making a big mistake.

**REPORTER:** And you, miss? What's your opinion?

**WOMAN 2:** Well, I think the building is a good idea. We need new business to come to our city, and a lot of people like to work in a new building. I agree with the city.

**REPORTER:** Thank you very much.

**B. REPORTER:** Now, for my second question. Excuse me, ma'am. City High School said that they didn't have money, and they stopped all music classes. What do you think about that?

**WOMAN 3:** Well, I was shocked and angry! I didn't want the school to stop the music classes. My child loved them.

**REPORTER:** And you, sir? What do you think?

**MAN 2:** I disagree with her. The school needed to stop some classes. And students don't need to learn music!

**REPORTER:** Thank you very much. That's my report for today. See you next week.